WOMEN TRAVELERS
ON THE NILE

WOMEN TRAVELERS
ON THE NILE

An Anthology of Travel Writing
through the Centuries

Edited by
Deborah Manley

The American University in Cairo Press
Cairo   New York

Copyright © 2016 by
The American University in Cairo Press
113 Sharia Kasr el Aini, Cairo, Egypt
420 Fifth Avenue, New York, NY 10018
www.aucpress.com

Exclusive distribution outside Egypt and North America by I.B.Tauris & Co Ltd.,
6 Salem Road, London, W2 4BU

Dar el Kutub No. 25917/15
ISBN 978 977 416 787 4

Dar el Kutub Cataloging-in-Publication Data

Manley, Deborah
    Women Travelers on the Nile: An anthology of travel writing through
    the centuries/ Deborah Manley—Cairo: The American University in Cairo
    Press, 2016.
        p.   cm.
        ISBN 978 977 416 787 4
        1.   Egypt—History—20thCentury
    962

1 2 3 4 5   20 19 18 17 16

Project editor: Rawan Abdel Latif
Designed by Fatiha Bouzidi
Printed in the United States of America

Contents

Cairo **23**

The Environs of Cairo **49**

Introduction

"I quite agree with Miss Martineau that one of the greatest nuisances in travelling is keeping a journal. One is far more disposed to lie down and rest after a fatiguing ride of eight or nine hours on a camel, beneath a burning sun; than— having made a hasty toilette—to take out one's writing materials. I persevered, however, and rejoice that I did so."

—Lady Tobin, 1853

Most men set out to travel with a purpose—for many their purpose was, and is, related to work rather than leisure. In the past women needed a purpose to justify their travels more than did men—for, unless they had enough money of their own, they had to ask for either male or female permission. Some women travelers were invited to make up numbers in a group or to accompany their husbands, but then quite often wrote a book of their travels—and thus became the traveler still remembered, while the men of their party are remembered only as a presence.

One of the great differences between the female and male travelers was that women could meet the women of Egypt. Some of the women started as 'travelers' but then lived in Egypt for several years, and would have spoken Arabic and thus have had further insights into Egyptian life. Sarah Belzoni came with her husband but spent much time independent from him. Mary Whately, teacher and missionary in Egypt from the 1870s, met both the poorest women along the Nile and the richest women in the harems of Cairo. Sophia Poole, sister of the famous Edward Lane, lived among the women of Cairo for many years—and became an object of other travelers' interest in her own right.

I have myself been privileged to travel up the Nile on a modern-day *dahabiya* similar to those on which most of the women traveled, and I can understand fully the pleasures they had and the Egypt they saw and brought to us in their writings.

Alexandria, the Delta,
and Suez

Before the days of flight, travelers to Egypt arrived at Alexandria or one of the Suez Canal ports, crossing the desert to Cairo and the Nile. Alexandria was for many travelers

their first experience of Egypt and, after a journey down the Nile, the flat coastline at Alexandria was their last sight of the country.

What You Need to Bring, 1861
M.L.M. Carey

The Arabs wash well enough, but the iron is beyond them; and therefore the choice for Europeans must frequently be between a lady's-maid, a couple of irons for their own use, or doing without an iron at all.

With no more than the usual stock of linen required at home; a few *common* dresses for the river; the lightest possible shawl or mantle for the daytime; plenty of warm wraps for the night; round hats, neckhandkerchiefs, veils, gauntleted gloves, and large, lined umbrellas, to guard the white skin against the unscrupulous burning of the Egyptian sun; two pair of strong boots for the desert and temple excursions; light ones to baffle mosquitoes at all hours of the day; galoshes, for the mud on the banks of the Nile; elder-flower water for the eyes and the complexion; a preparation of zinc—one grain to ten drops of water—one drop of which applied to the corner of the eye on the point of a fine camel's-hair brush, and repeated night and morning, is an *infallible cure* on the first symptoms of the dreaded Ophthalmia; a large quantity of quassia, to destroy the flies; thermometers and guide books—Murray, Wilkinson, Warburton, etc; and, finally, as there are no M.D.s on the Nile, a good book and a box of medicines—homoeopathic, of course—we considered ourselves armed against all emergencies.

There is an art in arranging mosquito curtains, as in everything else, and if it is not well understood, these protections are useless. When properly gathered round on the frame round the top of the bed, no mosquitoes can penetrate during the day. A short time before retiring to rest, a vigorous flapping with a fly-flapper or towel should be resorted to, the curtains instantly dropped and carefully tucked in all round. If one small aperture is left, farewell to sleep! Although the Arab servants are supposed to go through these manoeuvres in a masterly style, we always found it necessary to repeat them again for ourselves just before getting into bed. In this last operation, too, unless you are very expert and expeditious, the mosquitoes are on the watch, and will be sure to accompany you. At about sunset these little tormentors of our race congregate upon the window-panes in large numbers. A few moments spent in destroying them at this time will be well repaid. The slightest stroke of a handkerchief puts an end to their fragile existence, and renders that of the traveller so much the more endurable for one day.

Arriving in Egypt, 1779
Eliza Fay

23rd July, 1779 We are now off Alexandria, which makes a fine appearance from the sea on a near approach; but being built on low ground, is, as the seamen say "very difficult to hit." We were two days almost abreast of the Town. There is a handsome Pharos or light-house in the new harbour, and it is in all respects far preferable; but no vessels belonging to Christians can anchor there, so we were forced to go into the old one, of which however we escaped the dangers, if any exist. . . .

Having mounted our asses, the use of horses being forbidden to any but musselmans, we sallied forth preceded by a Janizary, with his drawn sword, about three miles over a sandy desert, to see Pompey's Pillar, esteemed to be the finest column in the World. This pillar which is exceedingly lofty, but I have no means of ascertaining its exact height, is composed of three blocks of Granite; (the pedestal, shaft, and capital, each containing one). When we consider the immense weight of the granite, the raising such masses, appear beyond the powers of man. Although quite unadorned, the proportions are so exquisite, that it must strike every beholder with a kind of awe, which softens into melancholy, when one reflects that the renowned Hero whose name it bears, was treacherously murdered on this very Coast, by the boatmen who were conveying him to Alexandria; while his wretched wife stood on the vessel he had just left, watching his departure, as we may naturally suppose, with inexpressible anxiety. What must have been her agonies at the dreadful event! Though this splendid memorial bears the name of Pompey, it is by many supposed to have been erected in memory of the triumph, gained over him at the battle of Pharsalia.

Leaving more learned heads than mine to settle this disputed point, let us proceed to ancient Alexandria, about a league from the modern town; which presents to the eye an instructive lesson on the instability of all sublunary objects. This once magnificent City, built by the most famous of all Conquerors, and adorned with the most exquisite productions of art, is now little more than a heap of Ruins; yet the form of the streets can still be discerned; they were regular, and many of the houses (as I recollect to have read in Athens) had fore-courts bounded by dwarf walls, so much in the manner of our Lincoln's-Inn Fields, that the resemblance immediately struck me.

Entering Alexandria, 1842
Sophia Poole

The old or western harbour of Alexandria (anciently called Eunostos Portus) is deeper and more secure than the new harbour (which is called Magnus Portus). The former, which was once exclusively appropriated to the vessels of Muslims, is now open to the ships of all nations; and the latter, which was "the harbour of the infidels," is almost deserted. The entrance of the old harbour is rendered difficult by reefs of rocks, leaving three natural passages, of which the central has the greatest depth of water. The rocks occasion a most unpleasant swell, from which we all suffered, but I especially; and I cannot describe how gratefully I stepped on shore, having passed the smooth water of the harbour. Here already I see so much upon which to remark, that I must indulge myself by writing two or three letters before our arrival in Cairo, where the state of Arabian society being unaltered by European innovations, I hope to observe much that will interest you with respect to the condition of the native female society.

The streets, until we arrived at the part of the town inhabited by Franks, were so narrow that it was extremely formidable to meet anything on our way. They are miserably close, and for the purpose of shade the inhabitants have in many cases thrown matting from roof to roof, extending across the street, with here and there a small aperture to admit light; but the edges of these apertures are generally broken, and the torn matting hanging down: in short, the whole appearance is gloomy and wretched. I ought not, however, to complain of the narrowness of the streets, for where the sun is excluded by the matting, the deep shade produced by the manner in which the houses are constructed is most welcome in this sunny land; and, indeed, when we arrived at the Frank part of the town, which is in appearance almost European, and where a wide street and a fine open square form a singular contrast to the Arab part of the town, we scarcely congratulated ourselves; for the heat was intense, and we hastened to our hotel, and gratefully enjoyed the breeze which played through the apartments. . . .

The windows of our hotel command a view of the great square, and I can scarcely describe to you the picturesque attraction of the scene. Among the various peculiarities of dress, feature, and complexion, which characterize the nature of Africa and the East, none are more striking than those which distinguish the noble and hardy western Bedawee, enveloped as he is in his ample woollen shirt, or hooded cloak, and literally clothed suitably for a Russian winter. You will believe that my attention has been directed to the veiled women, exhibiting in their dull disguise no other attraction than a degree of stateliness in their carriage, and a remarkable beauty in their large dark eyes, which, besides being sufficiently distinguished by nature, are rendered more conspicuous by the black border of kohl round the lashes, and by the concealment of the rest of the features. The cameldrivers' cries "O'a," "Guarda,"and "Sakin," resound every where, and at every moment, therefore, you may imagine the noise and confusion in the streets . . .

We saw little worthy of remark until we reached the Obelisks, which are situated at an angle of the enclosure, almost close to the shore of the new harbour; I mean those obelisks called Cleopatra's Needles. Each is composed of a single rock of red granite, nearly seventy feet in length, and seven feet and a half wide at the base. And here I wondered, as so many have done before me, that the ancient Egyptians contrived to raise such solid masses, and concluded that their knowledge of machinery, of which they have left such extraordinary proofs, must have been remarkable indeed.

The Pasha's Palace, 1861
M.L.M. Carey

The Palace is situated near the entrance of the Harbour. Its rooms are very handsomely furnished and hung with damask, and the floors beautifully inlaid with different kinds of wood. They are for the most part staterooms, in which the Pasha receives his own and foreign officers, and visitors. Our guide Mohammed's version was, that in one he "held his Parliament," in another his "Church," and in a third he showed the divan upon which he reposes for a time after dinner, leaning back against one pillow, whilst two other very large ones are placed in front, upon each of which, Mohamed said, one leg reclines, "*because he is so fat.*" And this was uttered in a tone of intense admiration! The chandeliers in two of the apartments are magnificent, and come from Paris; indeed, all the decorations are of French workmanship. The Hareem is close by: and the ladies walk in the surrounding garden. The Pashas are allowed four wives by the Koran, but Mohammed told us confidentially that they owned about sixty or seventy.

Women of the Delta, 1827
Anne Katherine Elwood

In our walks, the women in the villages, and on the banks, eyed us with the most intense curiosity. Some of them were much ornamented with gold, and their veils were tied up between the eyes with a string of small silver bells. Their chief occupation appeared to be the drawing and carrying of water; the children, generally in a complete state of nature, were frequently much frightened at our appearance, and one of them, on meeting us, ran quickly away, crying out "Mamma, Mamma," in as broad a tone as any Scotch boy could have done.

The men laughed good-naturedly, but not disrespectfully at our foreign appearance, and turned away their eyes, exclaiming, "Haram!" One morning I found myself suddenly caught hold of, and turning, in some degree of alarm, I beheld a woman in the blue dress of the country, completely veiled, offering her hand, and exclaiming, at the utmost pitch of her voice, "Salamat! Salamat!" I returned the salutation, and gave her my hand in return, upon which she made signs for me to follow her to her house, in a village at a little distance, but I was afraid of accompanying her, as the invitation did not extend to C. [Anne's husband]. She, however, offered her hand to him in a very friendly manner, and seemed very well pleased at his putting some piastres into it.

Alexandria to the Nile, 1849
Florence Nightingale

Here we are, our second step in Egypt. We left Alexandria on the 25th [November] at 7 o'clock a.m. We were towed up the Mahmoudieh Canal by a little steam-tug to Atfeh, which we reached at 5 p.m. The canal perfectly uninteresting; the day gloomy. I was not very well so stayed below from Alexandria to Cairo. At Atfeh, we were seventy people on board a boat built for twenty-five . . . Then first I saw the solemn Nile, flowing gloomily; a ray of sun shining out of the cloudy horizon from the setting sun upon him. He was still very high [during the inundation]; the current rapid. The solemnity is not produced by sluggishness, but by the dark colour of the water, and enormous unvarying character of the flat plain, a fringe of date trees here and there, nothing else. By six o'clock p.m. we were off, the moon shining, and the stars all out.

On board our steamer, where there is no sleeping place but a ladies' cabin, where you sit round all night, nine to the square yard, we have hardly any English, no Indians, for fortunately it is not the transit week. Our condition is not improved physically, for the boat is equally full of children, screaming all night, and the children are much fuller of vermin; but mentally it is, for the screams are Egyptian, Greek, Italian and Turkish screams and the fleas, etc. are Circassian, Chinese and Coptic fleas.

First Sight of the Pyramids, 1846
Harriet Martineau

Till 3 p.m. there was little variety in the scenery. I was most struck with the singular colouring;—the diversity

of browns. There was the turbid river, of vast width, roll-
ing between earthy banks; and on these banks were mud
villages, with their conical pigeon-houses. The minarets
and the Sheikhs' tombs were fawn-coloured and white;
and the only variety of these shades of the same colour
was in the scanty herbage, which was so coarse as to be
almost of no colour at all. But the distinctness of outline,
the glow of the brown, and the vividness of light and
shade, were truly a feast to the eye. At 3 o'clock, when
approaching Werdán, we saw spreading acacias growing

out of the dusty soil; and palms were clustered thickly about the town; and at last we had something beyond the banks to look at—a sandy ridge which extends from Tunis to the Nile.

When we had passed Werdán, about 4 p.m., Mr E. came to me with a mysterious countenance, and asked me if I should like to view the Pyramids. We stole past the groups of careless talkers, and went to the bows of the boat, where I was mounted on boxes and coops, and shown where to look. In a minute I saw them, emerging from behind a sand hill. They were very small; for we were still twenty-five miles from Cairo; but there could be no doubt about them for a moment; so sharp and clear were the light and shadow on the two sides we saw.

I had been assured that I should be disappointed in the first sight of the Pyramids; and I had maintained that I could not be disappointed, as of all the wonders of the world, this is the most literal, and, to the dweller among mountains, like myself, the least imposing. I now found both my informant and myself mistaken. So far from being disappointed, I was filled with surprise and awe: and so far was I from having anticipated what I saw, that I felt as if I had never before looked upon anything so new as those clear and vivid masses, with their sharp blue shadows, standing firm and alone on their expanse of sand.

In a few minutes, they appeared to grow wonderfully larger; and they looked lustrous and most imposing in the evening light. This impression of the Pyramids was never fully renewed. I admired them every evening from my window at Cairo; and I took the surest means of convincing myself of their vastness, by going to the top of the largest; but this first view of them was the most moving: and I cannot think of it without emotion.

Between this time and sunset, the most remarkable thing was the infinity of birds. I saw a few pelicans and many cormorants; but the flocks—I might say the shoals—of wild ducks and geese which peopled the air, gave me a stronger impression of the wildness of the country, the foreign character of the scenery, than anything I had yet seen.

Toward Cairo and Arriving, 1855
Lady Tobin

The sun rose in all his glory the following day upon a lovely scene. Scarcely a cloud was in the sky, the Nile was covered with boats and rafts, and many fine palms and sycamores grew on either bank, some of which reared their tall heads out of the river, so high was the inundation. The small towns with their minarets, and the mud villages, looked most picturesque as we approached them, but were sadly disappointing in reality. Their inhabitants seemed poor and wretched in the extreme, and the children ran around quite naked.

On Wednesday, October 12th, the Pyramids were in sight. Wonderful and mysterious creations! They stood distinct in the desert before us. No other object was there to turn our attention from their clear outlines. We were not even in motion, for the wind had become directly contrary.

As we approached the capital, the scenery became more and more interesting. The palace of Shoobra was pointed out to us on our left. At noon we came to anchor at Boulak, the port of Cairo, and immediately despatched Antonio to secure donkeys. He soon returned with the number required, and we were thereby enabled to mount them without being torn in pieces by rival competitors.

We ladies found ourselves ill at ease on the Arab saddles just at first; but speedily learnt to think them as comfortable as any others, though not so safe—according to *our* mode of riding—as they are for Egyptian women, who sit astride upon them.

Cairo

The great, sprawling city of Cairo has always amazed the traveler—with its beauty, with the crush of humanity through its narrow, winding streets and, later, along the great boulevards, with its amazing variety. The travelers—in

the past—enjoyed the markets, visited the ladies of the har-
ems, ventured into the baths, and looked onward up the
Nile where they were to travel.

Arriving from the Desert, 1844
Countess Hahn Hahn

I found myself again upon the old and too-well-known
desert plain. How long and how broad it is, Heaven only
knows—with again single cultivated spots to the right,
and to the left also, again, nothing but the accustomed
mountain-chain of Arabia, which bears the name Mokkatam. It must be said, however, that the plain was no
longer deserted by man. The villagers were carrying to
the city oranges and lemons, dates and bananas; whilst
from the latter were issuing travellers, traders and merchants, trains of camels and asses, soldiers exercising
their horses—in short, the further we proceeded the
more apparent became the traffic that generally prevails
in the neighbourhood of a large city. At length carriages
too! Folks driving in European fashion! What an unusual
sight! In a small *drosky,* Ibrahim Pasha; in a *coupé* with

four horses, Abbas Pasha! Running footmen were in front—a fashion now quite extinct in Europe.

On the declivity of the Mokkatam rises the citadel, the palace of the ruler of Egypt; at its feet lies the great, great city, with its obedient people. A multitude of elegant minarets shot distinctly aloft out of the indistinct throng of habitations which are surrounded, and, as it were, grown over with palms and other trees. In the foreground a row of windmills, elevated upon sandhills, present their ungraceful forms; and single large monuments disengage themselves from the multitude of tombs visible in the extensive burying-grounds. But in the background, on the other side of the city, are one or two mighty structures. Are they hills?—They are too regular. Are they buildings? They are too gigantic. They are the pyramids of Gizeh. They command and domineer over the picture, and attract the gaze with a magnetic power. And with justice. Like the pictures of a family in a great ancestral hall, do they begin the series of development which the human race passes through in that sphere in which the intellectual idea envelopes itself in a sensual garment, in order to make the impression which we call Art. In these creations must original faculties have been active; not material only—but also spiritual.

So Much for an Artist to See, 1899
E.M. Merrick

It was always a moving scene, and the novelty of dresses and faces perfectly enchanting. But when I went into the bazaars I was even more charmed, and could quite agree with one of the Royal Academicians, who told me I should find a picture at every corner. I made many rapid sketches there, and often before I could reach my room with them on return to the hotel they were sold. Water-carriers, with their quaint water-skins and brass cups, which they banged together; Bedouins on their camels; donkeys, with attendant donkey-boys—I made them all sit for their portraits, with more or less success. And in making sketches in Cairo I nearly always found the Arabs kind and courteous, anxious to lend me a chair; and sometimes, in the bazaars, inviting me to sit inside

their little shops out of the way of the inquisitive crowd which always gathered round, and bringing me a cup of Persian tea or coffee. "Backsheesh" was very often asked if I was suspected of making a sketch of one of them, but they always were amused and laughed if I suggested they should give *me* "backsheesh" for painting *them.*

The Scene from My Balcony, 1907

Norma Lorimer

However long I stay in Cairo, this quarter of the Ezbe-
kiyeh will always maintain a paramount place in my
vision of the city. It is so strange, so picturesque, so
unceasingly amusing, so changingly changing, so simple
and yet so depraved. For the first three days I thought I
should never leave my balcony. Why should I? Here was
the most delightful feast of colour and oriental happen-
ings you could ever hope to find. Here the Egypt of the
Pyramids, the Egypt of the tombs of the kings and of the
Sphinx, was forgotten—and the city of the Caliphs did
not matter. Let them wait; here was the East, the East I
loved the most, the East of poverty and simplicity. . . .

How could I ever tire of watching the life that flows
and loiters along that wide pavement? The wall is broad
enough to afford on its flat top excellent quarters for
the stock-in-trade of the various merchants, who sell
anything from Roman Catholic church bric-a-brac
to exquisite Oriental embroideries, whose value they
know less about than the quality or use of the European

trousers and coats that hang from the points of the high railings. You have to leave the pavement now and then, for decency will not allow you to disturb the circle of brown-limbed donkey-boys—as slim and active in their one white garment as the athletes of old Greece—who squat around a circular tray raised a few feet from the ground, covered with tempting viands.

Countless little blue bowls full of various pickles and savoury morsels cover the round table, which is always arranged with a fascinating delicacy and refinement. Each customer buys a piece of bread from the bread vendor close by, who carries a stack of it on his head with the balance of an acrobat. It is scone-shaped, but so raised in the baking that it is quite hollow inside; he makes a pouch of it by tearing an opening in it, and then selects from each blue bowl a morsel of what his stomach most desires. The *bonnes bouches* are stowed away in the bread pocket, to be eaten at leisure.

Passing in the Streets, 1852
Ida Pfeiffer

Many of the streets were so narrow, that when loaded camels meet, one party must always be led into a by-street until the others had passed. In these narrow lanes I continually encountered crowds of passengers, so that I really felt quite anxious, and wondered how I should find my way through. People mounted on horses and donkeys tower above the moving mass; but the asses themselves appear like pigmies beside the high, lofty-looking camels, which do not lose their proud demeanour even under their heavy burdens. Men often slip by under the heads of the camels. The riders keep as close as possible to the houses, and the mass of pedestrians winds dexterously between. There are water-carriers, vendors of goods, numerous blind men groping their way with sticks, and bearing baskets with fruit, bread, and other provisions for sale; numerous children, some of them running about the streets, and others playing before the house-doors; and lastly, the Egyptian ladies, who ride on asses

to pay their visits, and come in long processions with their children and negro servants.

Let the reader further imagine the cries of the vendors, the shouting of the drivers and passengers, the terrified screams of flying women and children, the quarrels which frequently arise, and the peculiar noisiness and talkativeness of these people, and he can fancy what an effect this must have on the nerves of a stranger. I was in mortal fear at every step, and on reaching home in the evening felt quite unwell; but as I never once saw an accident occur, I at length accustomed myself to the hubbub, and could follow my guide where the crowd was thickest without feeling uneasy.

The streets, or as they may be properly called, the lanes of Cairo are splashed with water several times in a day; fountains and large vessels of water are also placed every where for the convenience of the passers-by. In the broad streets straw-mats are hung up to keep off the sun's rays.

The population of Cairo is estimated at 200,000, and is a mixed one, consisting of Arabs, Mamelukes, Turks,

Berbers, Negroes, Bedouins, Christians, Greeks, Jews, etc. Thanks to the powerful arm of Mehemet Ali, they all live peacefully together.

The City at Night, 1870
Mary Whately

Formerly each district of the city had an arched doorway to the chief of the narrow little streets of the quarter, and a huge massive wooden door, which was locked after a certain hour at night; and if by a rare chance I had been to see friends, and was returning after ten o'clock, my servant had to arouse the doorkeeper, who was asleep on a bench beside this great door, and get him to unlock it; often a quarter of an hour was spent in waking him up and waiting by persons who returned late. Many of these doors are now taken away in the making of the new streets, and the largest thoroughfares in the city (though only these) are lighted now with gas. Formerly we had to take a lamp if going out even the shortest distance after sunset; but even now it is needful if going to a wedding, for instance, or any visit to a native family out of the broad highway.

The little old-fashioned lamps were of prepared paper or calico, made to fold up flat and go in a man's pocket, a piece of wax taper being carried with them. These are still found, but glass lanterns are more common with persons of the better sort, who generally make a servant (or slave boy if they are natives) walk in front carrying it. In the narrow lanes of a great part of the city, where rubbish is always found, and where the half-wild dogs are crouching about among the dust-heaps, and stones encumber the path, it is necessary to pick the way very carefully if walking at night, and the lamp is usually held as *low* as possible, in order to throw light on the path for a few steps before the person walking. This is no doubt an old custom. Formerly, when no gas was found in Egypt, I used to watch from my window in the city passengers returning home in the short winter evenings, and each one carrying his lantern, or his servant, if a rich man, holding it before his feet, and think of the comparison in the Psalm, "Thy word is a light unto my *feet* and a lantern to my *path."* Just light for the way, step by step, is all we expect as the little lantern throws its ray on the rough footpath . . .

Our Neighbours, 1863
Lucie Duff Gordon

The street and the neighbours would divert you. Opposite lives a Christian dyer who must be a seventh brother of the admirable barber. The same impertinence, loquacity, and love of meddling in everyone's business. I long to see him thrashed, though he is a constant comedy. My delightful servant, Omar Abou-el-Hallaweh (the father of sweets)—his family are pastry cooks—is the type of all the amiable *jeune premiers* of the stories. I am privately of opinion that he is Bedr-ed-Deen Hassan, the more that he can make cream tarts and there is no pepper in them. Cream tarts are not very good, but lamb stuffed with pistachio nuts fulfils all one's dreams of excellence. The Arabs next door and the Levantines opposite are quiet enough, but how *do* they eat all the cucumbers they buy of the man who cries them every morning as "fruit gathered by sweet girls in the garden with the early dew."

The more I see of the back-slums of Cairo, the more in love I am with it. The oldest European towns are tame and regular in comparison, and the people are so pleasant. If you smile at anything that amuses you, you get the kindest, brightest smile in person; they give hospitality with their faces, and if one brings out a few words, "Mashallah! what Arabic the Sitt Ingleez speaks." The Arabs are clever enough to understand the amusement of a stranger and to enter into it, and amused in turn, and they are wonderfully unprejudiced. When Omar explains to me their views on various matters, he adds: "The Arab people think so—I know not if right," and the way in which the Arab merchants worked the electric telegraph, and the eagerness of the Fellaheen for steam-ploughs, are quite extraordinary. They are extremely clever and nice children, easily amused, easily roused into a fury which lasts five minutes and leaves no malice, and half the lying and cheating of which they are accused comes from misunderstanding and ignorance.

Processions Past the Window, 1842
Sophia Poole

The wedding processions, in which the poor bride walks under a canopy of silk, not only veiled, but enveloped in a large shawl, between two other females, amuse me much; while the tribe before the 'destined one' occasionally demonstrate their joy by executing many possible, and, to our ideas, many impossible feats, and the rear is brought up by the contributions of children from many of the houses *en route*. The bride must, indeed, be nearly suffocated long before she reaches her destination, for she has to walk, frequently almost fainting, under a midday sun, sometimes a long distance, while a few musicians make what is considered melody with drums and shrill hautboys, and attending females scream their *zaghareet* (or quavering cries of joy), in deafening discord in her train.

The funeral processions distress me. The corpse of a man is carried in an open bier, with merely a shawl thrown over the body, through which the form is painfully visible. The body of a woman is carried in a covered bier over which a shawl is laid, and an upright piece of wood, covered also with a shawl and decorated with ornaments belonging to the female head-dress, rises from the forepart. The corpses of children are carried on this latter kind of bier.

One sound that I heard as a funeral procession approached, I can never forget; it was a cry of such deep sorrow—a sob of such heartfelt distress, that it was clearly distinguished from the wail of the hired women who joined the funeral chorus. We were immediately drawn to the windows, and saw a man leading a procession of women, and bearing in his arms a little dead infant, wrapt merely in a shawl, and travelling to its last earthly home. The cry of agony proceeded, I conclude, from its mother, and could only be wrung from a nearly bursting heart. Contend against me who may, I must ever maintain my opinion, that no love is so deep, no attachment so strong, as that of mother to child, and of child to mother.

Khan El-Khaleelee, 1842
Sophia Poole

Khán El-Khaleelee, which is situated in the centre of that part which constituted the original city, a little to the east of the main street, and occupies the site of the cemetery of the Fawátim (the Khaleefehs of Egypt), particularly deserves to be mentioned, being one of the chief marts of Cairo. It consists of a series of short lanes, with several turnings, and has four entrances from different quarters.

The shops in this khán are mostly occupied by Turks, who deal in readymade clothes and other articles of dress, together with arms of various kinds, the small prayer-carpets used by the Muslims, and other commodities. Public auctions are held there (as in many other markets in Cairo) twice in the week, on Monday and Thursday, on which occasions the khan is so crowded, that, in some parts, it is difficult for a passenger to push his way through. The sale begins early in the morning, and lasts till the noon-prayers. Clothes (old as well as new), shawls, arms, pipes, and a variety of other goods, are offered for sale in this manner by brokers, who carry them up and down the market. Several water-carriers, each with a goat-skin of water on his back, and a brass cup for the use of any one who would drink, attend on these occasions. Sherbet of raisins, and bread (in round, flat cakes), with other eatables, are also cried up and down the market; and on every auction day, several real or pretended idiots, with a distressing number of other beggars, frequent the khán.

Beautiful Architecture, 1907
Norma Lorimer

These Mameluke houses of old Cairo have no rivals in Oriental domestic architecture, or in fairy elegance and fantastic grace. In many of them the walls of the best apartments, where the master of the house entertains his men friends, still gleam with the iridescence of old Persian tiles, and jewel-inlaid fountains still delight the ear with the splash of falling water.

Some of these palaces of pleasure have fallen upon evil days; I have seen one high room which any one can find for the looking, for it is near the famous Blue Mosque, so blessed with every grace that Saracenic art could bestow upon it, that a little lump rose to my throat when I suddenly entered it from the dark and disorderly staircase I had climbed to reach it. The mixture of desolation and beauty was overwhelming—cocks and hens and large-eared Persian rabbits were scattered about the floor.

Gems of stained glass still glowed like uncut jewels from the lace-work of white stucco which ran in a deep frieze along the top of the brown meshrebiyeh windows, which formed one side of the gigantic apartment. Not a particle of it had been disturbed by impious hands, not one screen of the priceless meshrebiyeh had been cut out for sale—the place had been allowed to slowly drift into ruin. The youth who showed me over it said he had no money to spend upon restoring a house which was ten times larger than he could afford to use; he seemed to have no money to do more than keep body and soul together, from his delicate appearance; yet he stiffened with pride when I suggested that he should let off one or two of the splendid old rooms of the palace to wealthy Americans. . . . He scorned the idea with as much hauteur as though his one cotton garment had been the richest brocade, and his palace guarded by an army of slaves.

The Cotton Bazaar and the Water-carriers, 1914
E.L. Butcher

Very few visitors seem to know the cotton bazaar in Cairo, yet it is well worth a visit, not only because it is a very picturesque, if insanitary, place, but because it is one of the few almost perfect examples left in Cairo of a khan for travellers. In just such a place as this Our Saviour must have been born at Bethlehem. There is the court for the animals, all driven in and herded here for the night in the days long ago, when the khan was used for its original purpose, and all round are deep arched recesses, with stone platforms in front of them, where the herdsmen and servants in charge of the animals slept. Above this and all round it, with an awning or light roof to the court, ran the rooms of the inn proper looking into the court. The only entrance to the place is through a low, narrow, arched way, which leads from the court, under the inn, to the street.

Now the arched recesses are filled with brightly coloured cottons—stripes for the men only, other patterns for the women. I discovered once that my servants were rather scandalized because I had bought myself a dress of the striped cotton which should only be worn by men. On the platforms sit the merchants with their scribes.

Behind the cotton bazaar the weavers of silk ends to cotton cloths may be seen at their work. There are many qualities of Egyptian silks; the best is very expensive, but the tourists generally buy a quality which, though half cotton, has the merit of washing well to the last. It is always woven in fine stripes, and generally in beautiful colours.

Water-carriers are a very familiar sight in Cairo, though the modern water-carts have driven them from the principal streets. They fetch the water from the Nile to the houses where the women of the family are too well off to work in the fields, or go down with their jars to the river, and they still water some small streets where the carts cannot go. A favourite form of charity for the well-to-do is to set a zeyr outside his house for the benefit of thirsty passers-by, and this he pays a water carrier to keep full regularly. The water-sellers, too, are often hired by some rich man to dispense water gratuitously to every-one for the day, generally some day of feast.

The seller carries his supply in a zeyr upon his back, with a branch of green leaves by way of a stopper. He has two brass cups which he clinks together to attract attention. He generally carries a goolla also, and it is curious to watch the demeanour of one of these men in a crowd on an occasion when he has received a certain sum for the day, since he never asks nor waits for money.

The Bath, 1844
Sophia Poole

Whatever others may think of it, I confess that the operation of bathing in the Eastern manner is to me extremely agreeable; and I have found it singularly beneficial in removing the lassitude which is occasioned by the climate. It is true that it is followed by a sense of fatigue, but a delightful repose soon ensues; and the consequences, upon the whole, I find almost as enjoyable as the process itself.

The buildings containing the baths are all nearly on the same plan, and are much alike in appearance; the fronts being decorated fancifully, in red and white, and the interiors consisting of several apartments paved with marble. I will describe to you, in a few words, one of the best in Cairo, which I visited with three ladies of my acquaintance: English, Abyssinian, and Syrian.

After we had passed through two passages, we found ourselves in the first large apartment, or chamber of repose, in which the bathers undress previously to their entering the heated chambers, and in which they dress after taking the bath, and rest on a raised marble platform, or wide bench, on which are spread mats and carpets. . . . Each of us enveloped herself in a very long and broad piece of drapery—which, but for its size, I might call a scarf, and proceeded through a small chamber, which was moderately heated, to the principal inner apartment, where the heat was intense.

The plan of this apartment is that of a cross, having four recesses, each of which, as well as the central portion, is covered with a dome. The pavements are of black and white marble, and small pieces of fine red tile, very fancifully and prettily disposed. In the middle is a jet of hot water, rising from the centre of a high seat of marble, upon which many persons might sit together. . . .

On entering this chamber a scene presented itself which beggars description. My companions had prepared me for seeing many persons undressed; but imagine my astonishment in finding at least thirty women of all ages, and many young girls and children, perfectly unclothed. You will scarcely think it possible that no one but ourselves had a vestige of clothing. Persons of all colours, from the black and glossy shade of the negro to the fairest possible hue of complexion, were formed in groups, conversing as though full dressed, with perfect *nonchalance*, while others were strolling about, or sitting round the fountain. . . .

The first operation is a gentle kneading of the flesh, or champooing. Next the attendant cracks the joints of those who desire to submit to this process. I confess I did not suffer such an infliction. Some of the native women after this are rubbed with a rasp, or rather two rasps of different kinds, a coarse one for the feet, and a fine one for the body; but neither of these rasps do I approve. A small coarse woollen bag, into which the operator's hand is inserted, is in my opinion preferable.

Next the head and face are covered with a thick lather, which is produced by rubbing soap on a handful of fibres of the palm-tree, which are called *leef,* and which form a very agreeable and delicate looking rubber. It is truly ridiculous to see another under this operation. When her head and face have been well lathered, and the soap has been thoroughly washed off by abundance of hot water, a novice would suppose that at least *they* were sufficiently purified; but this is not the case: two or three such latherings, and as many washings, are necessary before the attendant thinks her duty to the head and face accomplished. Then follows the more agreeable part of the affair—the general lathering and rubbing, which is performed by the attendant so gently, and in so pleasant a manner, that it is quite a luxury; and I am persuaded that the Eastern manner of bathing is highly salubrious, from its powerful effect upon the skin.

When the operation was completed, I was enveloped in a dry piece of drapery, similar to the bathing-dress, and conducted to the reposing-room, where I was rubbed and dressed, and left to take rest and refreshment, and to reflect on the strange scene that I had witnessed.

The Environs of Cairo

From the great city travelers often took short expeditions out into the surrounding countryside to see the many sites close to Cairo.

The Tombs of the Mameluke Sultans, 1828
Sarah Lushington

The ultimate object of our excursion was the tombs of the Mameluke Sultans. These are situated, as it would appear, in the very heart of the Desert; and it struck me as one of the most singular features of Grand Cairo that, from the very centre of population, from a scene of luxuriant cultivation, we in a moment, without the slightest preparation, passed on to a plain and hills of sand. Not a tree, nor a habitation breaks the uniformity of the surface; nothing is visible but a district of graves, extending as far as the eye can reach; and, where the stones are no longer perceptible, little hillocks of sand mark the places of sepulture.

Amidst this desolation arise the tombs of the Mamelukes. The largest is that of Sultan Beerkook and his followers. It is in the form of a square, and its walls are in excellent preservation. On one side, in an arched and vaulted room inlaid with coloured marbles, are placed his remains; at the extremity of an open gallery is a similar room, now used as a mosque. The square is embellished with a minar and a dome. The latter especially, with the pulpit or muezzin, is cut in the most elegant and delicate fretwork stone.

The rest of the building was occupied by poor Arabs, who lived by begging, and in this dwelling are safe from tax and extortion.

The Pasha's Country Palace, 1828
Sarah Lushington

As I had already seen an Egyptian garden, I looked forward to an excursion to Shoobra, the country seat of the Pasha, with little or no curiosity. Proceeding, however, by a fine road, planted on each side with acacias and sycamores, whose growth, owing to the richness of the soil, kept pace with the impatient disposition of the Pasha, who had, at one sweep, cut down the avenue of mulberry trees three years before, we arrived at the house, which is situated close to the Nile, and commands a fine prospect of the river and city.

The exterior of the building exhibited nothing remarkable. On ascending a terrace a few feet square, we passed through a rough wooden door, such as is fit only for an outhouse, and found ourselves in the Pasha's room of audience. It was matted, and round the wall was fixed a row of cushions, on two corners of which were placed satin pillows, marking the seat the Pasha occupied according to the position of the sun. Just over a low ledge in the door, we stepped into a small room with a bedding on the floor; this was his sleeping chamber. Surely never monarch had so little luxury or state. Thence we came at once to the magnificent suite of apartments appropriated to the chief lady of the harem.

The centre of the principal room formed a sort of octagon, with three recesses, all inlaid with marble. From the four corners opened four small rooms, fitted with splendid divans and cushions of velvet, and cloth of gold; and a set of marble baths completed this series of elegant apartments.

The Pasha's Garden at Shoobra, 1853
Lady Tobin

We rode to Shoobra on the afternoon of Friday, December 23rd, along a wide avenue of acacia trees, the favourite *promenade* of Cairo. The distance is four miles from the Bab-el-Hadid, which is pointed out as a place famous as the scene of a fierce encounter between Richard I and Salah-e-deen, and where there are the remains of very ancient walls.

The road gradually approached the Nile as we advanced towards the village of Shoobra, and at last ran close along the river's bank. Arrived at the outer gate of the royal pleasure grounds, where are the Pasha's stables, we dismounted; and at the end of a short avenue came to a second portal, with a very shabby lodge attached to it. The gardens are extensive, and most beautifully kept.

Chrysanthemums, roses, geraniums, and several of our greenhouse plants were in blossom; the weeping willow and the pomegranate were to be seen here and there; but the principal growth was that of the orange, lemon and citrus. One of the gardeners gave us bouquets of flowers; and some oranges, like those of Malta, produced by grafting upon the pomegranate trees.

The broad straight walks radiate from centres, and some of them are covered overhead with trellis work. We startled a pretty gazelle from under some trees. The Octagon Pagoda of gaily coloured glass cost 7,000 purses—the *kees* (purse) being equivalent to £5 sterling. Its interior is fitted up as a saloon, in the centre of which is a bronze fountain, and also a candelabra of carved wood. The floor is curiously inlaid, and the part that immediately surrounds the fountain forms a circular pattern of crescents and stars. The next object of attraction was the Great Fountain *Kiosk,* or according to our guide, the Pacha's *Divan.* The erection of a gas-house for supplying the lamps has ruined the general effect of the building. An enormous marble *reservoir,* containing water four feet in depth, is surrounded by balustrades, which, as well as the columns and mouldings of the open corridors—are from Carrara, and were worked by Italians. At each of the four corners is an apartment fitted up with divans; the first we entered had a painted ceiling, plate glass windows, and splendid silk hangings; the floor and panelled walls were of inlaid wood. The framework of the chairs and tables—for there was a mixture of the European with the Oriental style—struck us as being exceedingly paltry, compared with all around them, and their own rich damask coverings. Another of these rooms contained a billiard table, and in a third was a full length portrait of Mohammed Ali—considered an excellent likeness.

Ascending the Pyramid, 1845
Harriet Martineau

On looking up, it was not the magnitude of the Pyramid which made me think it scarcely possible to achieve the ascent, but the unrelieved succession—almost infinite—of bright yellow steps; a most fatiguing image! Three strong and respectable looking Arabs now took me in charge. One of them, seeing me pin up my gown in front, that I might not stumble over it, gave me his services as lady's maid. He turned up my gown all round, and tied it in a most squeezing knot, which lasted all through the enterprise.

We set out from the north-eastern corner. By far the most formidable part of the ascent was the first six or eight blocks. If it went on to the top thus broken and precipitous, the ascent would, I feel, be impossible. Already, it was disagreeable to look down, and I was much out of breath. One of my Arabs carried a substantial camp-stool, which had been given to me in London with a view to this very adventure—that it might divide the higher steps—some of which being four feet high, seem impracticable enough beforehand. But I found it better to trust to the strong and steady lifting of the Arabs in such places, and, above everything, not to stop at all, if possible; or, if one must stop for breath, to stand with one's face to the Pyramid . . . The greatest part of one's weight is lifted by the Arabs at each arm; and when one comes to a four feet step, or a broken ledge, there is a third Arab behind.

I was agreeably surprised to find at the top, besides blocks standing up which gave us some shade, a roomy and even platform, where we might sit and write, and gaze abroad, and enjoy ourselves, without even seeing over the edge, unless we wished it.

In this northern direction, the green plain extends to the furthest horizon, and over to Cairo eastwards. It is dotted with villages—clusters of brown houses among palms—and watered with blue thread-like canals, and showing a faint line of causeway here and there. . . . In the midst of the sand, a train of camels, wonderfully diminutive, is winding along, and a few brown Arab tents are pitched, not far from the foot of the Pyramid.

Before the Sphynx, 1824
Anne Katherine Elwood

We came into the neighbourhood of the Sphynx; *the* Sphynx, of which everyone has heard so much, and here the soil presented some immense fissures, and such heavy beds of sand, that while wrapped no doubt in some very sublime speculation, down fell my donkey, and over its head went I—I was picked up by a Bedouin Arab, who was offering me some cucumbers and melons at the moment—but, though more frightened than hurt, this *contretemps* was enough to quell my courage for the day. However, that you do not attribute my fall to my bad riding, I beg to observe that several others of the party made a similar obeisance with myself to the Sphynx, by involuntarily prostrating themselves in the dust before her. The Sphynx presented an African countenance, and her hair was dressed much in the same style with my Nubian friends in the slave-market. The sand, which at times had been cleared away, has again collected, and it was at this time nearly embedded in it.

Up the Nile from Cairo

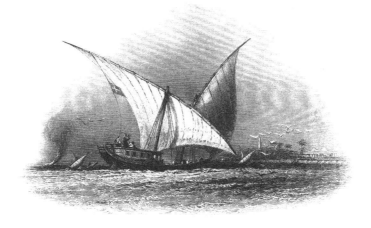

*Part of the exciting experience of visiting Cairo was the mak-
ing of arrangements for the journey southward on the Nile
to Nubia. This meant negotiating at the port of Bulaq for a
boat with a reis (or captain) and a crew. Then provisions had
to be laid in and various other arrangements had to be made.*

Our Dahabieh, 1844
Isabel Romer

These Dahabiehs are very graceful looking vessels, with two masts and three Lateen sails, and they are constructed with cabins for the accommodation of passengers which occupy the whole aft-part of the deck. Ours has two excellent cabins, fitted up at each side with Turkish divans, capable of being converted at night into four beds, and very neatly furnished with carpets and cushions, besides two book-shelves, well stocked with works of reference for Egyptian travellers. There is a *cabinette de toilette* beyond these, and in front is a tent or awning where the servants sleep; and I assure you that when all the doors are thrown open, our present abode has quite as consequential an appearance as many of the seaside lodging houses in England, where grand pianos are located, and quadrilles are danced in drawing rooms twelve feet long by ten.

Of course our bedding, linen, canteens and *batterie de cuisine* etc are supplied by ourselves, and Mohammed's perfect knowledge of the outfit required for such an excursion has saved us a world of trouble, and his cleverness and good management in providing everything that he knew to be adapted to English tastes and habits, has really not left us the possibility of forming a wish.

We had wisely prepared ourselves to expect a somewhat scrambling life of it, but most agreeably have we been surprised at finding everything going on under his auspices as smoothly as though we were in the best hotel on shore, and our table as well supplied as if the Marché St. Honoré were within his reach.

Our crew consists of a Reis, or captain, a pilot, and fourteen Arab sailors, besides which we have a Caireen cook, who is quite an artist, and our trusty interpreter Mohammed, making in all eighteen Mussulmans, to whose tender mercies we have consigned ourselves for the next six weeks.

A Prayer on Starting, 1842
Sophia Poole

A custom which is always observed by the Arab boat-men at the commencement of a voyage much pleased me. As soon as the wind had filled our large sail, the Reyyis (or captain of the boat) exclaimed, "El-Fat-hah." This is the title of the opening chapter of the Kur'an (a short and simple prayer), which the Reyyis and all the crew repeated together in a low tone of voice. Would to Heaven that, in this respect, the example of the poor Muslim might be followed by our countrymen, that our entire dependence on the protecting providence of God might be universally acknowledged, and every journey, and every voyage, be sanctified by prayer.

Our Boat from Luxor, 1827
Sarah Lushington

Our servant had the whole morning been cleaning the *maash* selected for us, from the mud and dirt, which adhered to it at least two inches thick. The outside had already dispelled any illusions I might have had of its resemblance to Cleopatra's galley, but when I entered it, I confess I was quite dismayed. A common coal barge on the river Thames would have afforded better accommodation. Two small cabins in the stern, the wooden partitions besmeared with dirt, every plank divided, some entirely broken out, admitting sun, wind, and rats, and the lowness of the ceiling, which did not allow of my standing upright, made me look round in hopeless discomfort.

Few minutes, however, elapsed before our tent was dismantled, the walls thrown over the top of the boat, and a projecting pole added, which, with the help of our trunks for a platform, and a carpet over them, formed a sort of verandah. We nailed table-cloths on the ceiling and sides of the cabin, and the openings most exposed to cold I closed with little coloured mats, which I happened to have brought with me from India. The carpet was spread; our two little brass camp beds soon looked like sofas, and it was no small gratification to me to see a clean, comfortable, nay, almost pretty habitation instead of the dirty dismal hole I had entered an hour before.

Met along the Way, 1875
Mary Whately

Almost every woman comes into market with a load on her head of some kind—either a pitcher of sour milk, or a *skin* of the same, with lumps of butter in it, or a basket of eggs or fowls, cheese or dates, leeks or onions, or any vegetables in season. There is little except provisions of a common kind, cattle etc, and a few coloured prints, and pieces of unbleached calico, thread, etc., sold in the market; scarcely anything of show or luxury, unless it be a few tiny looking-glasses, and clumsy combs, and red handkerchiefs in a corner. It is only in late years that a few plates and dishes are occasionally found in the houses of the wealthier farmers; the coarse red pottery of the country, made in a sort of pan, being the only earthen vessels in most village dwellings, and even these are not numerous. I used to wonder in those early days how they drank (not having spoon nor cup), till I saw them lift a pitcher of considerable weight (though much smaller than that carried on the head to *bring* water) and *pour* the draught from a height into their throats. I tried to do the same, but early habit being wanting, I only succeeded in watering my clothes plentifully, without getting more than a drop or two in the right direction.

The countrywomen are by no means as carefully veiled as the townspeople, and a great many of the poorer ones have no face-covering at all; but if they have to speak to a man, most will draw the muslin veil across the mouth and nose, holding it with one hand, or in the teeth, if both hands are busy weighing cheese or dates.

On the *S.S. Ramses the Great*, 1907
Norma Lorimer

It is delightful to think that we are going to do nothing all day today but enjoy the Nile—do nothing but feel the spell of Egypt—do nothing but sit under a shady awning, where a cool breeze always drifts from the bows of the boat, and watch the procession of Egypt pass along the green margin of the river's banks—do nothing but watch the fierce sunlight play on the amber sands. To be cool oneself and watch a hot world at work, what a luxury! what unconscious arrogance in the pleasure! yet is not enjoyment like all else merely relative? If there was nothing else to watch all day but the antics of our Soudanese crew, it would be sufficient for me. There is the ostrich-feather broom boy who watches for a speck of dust to brush away, and the brass boys who lift up rugs and mats to find some hidden treasure in the way of knobs to polish, indeed there is a boy with a grinning smile and flashing teeth for every mortal occupation you can imagine. I often wonder if there is a special crew kept to do nothing but say their prayers, for there is always a group of black-skinned Soudanese in white drawers on their knees in the bows of the boat. Perhaps Thomas Cook and Son recognise how valuable they are for "off days" on the Nile for tourists to kodak.

I was waked by the flush of the sunrise which flooded my room, and which called me to be up and doing—to watch the beginning of the new day.

It scarcely looked like a new day, except for its rosy, youthful light and the chill in the air, for all the world on the banks seemed to be doing exactly what it was doing last night when the lights went out; nothing had changed, it seemed as though only darkness had fallen over the land and had shut out all sights and sounds of man.

Meeting Crocodiles, 1845
Isabel Romer

Yesterday was marked by us with a white stone, as being the date of our first personal introduction to live crocodiles! I was summoned from my cabin to behold the monstrous reptiles basking on a bank of sand in the river; there were three of them—one enormously large—I should say at least fifteen feet long, and the two others evidently young things. A double-barrelled gun was immediately discharged at them, which caused the little ones to shuffle away into the water in a great fright; but the old fellow treated the salute with superb contempt, and after a second or two that showed he was accustomed to stand fire, waddled in leisurely after them, appearing to be quite conscious that the shot might have been fired at the citadel of Cairo with the same effect as against his own impenetrable scales.

Slaves on the Nile, 1827
Wolfradine Minutoli

Some days after we met several boats filled with negro slaves of both sexes, coming from Darfur and Sennaar, and laden besides with elephant's teeth, ostrich feathers, gold dust, parrots, etc. The people who are engaged in this traffic are called *gelaps*; they generally carry off children by force or by stratagem, and even frequently purchase them of the parents themselves. Not being accustomed to this sight, we felt at the view of these poor wretches, deprived of their liberty and forced from their native land, a sentiment of pity which would not have been so lively if we had known the state of destitution and misery which they experience in their own country.

The Turks are generally humane towards their slaves, who, besides, enjoy the protection of the laws in a special manner; for they have a right to demand to be resold whenever their condition becomes unhappy, and their masters venture to ill-treat them, which makes their situation almost equal to that of our servants in Europe. A great number of these negroes are employed in guarding the harems. The Pacha of Egypt, who is very magnificent in all his presents, sometimes sends several hundreds at once to the Grand Seignor. The negresses are particularly employed within doors; most of them are very intelligent, and learn with facility all sorts of female work.

The Europeans, who dare not have white slaves in Egypt, have now obtained the right of purchasing black ones; hence all the rich families at Cairo generally have some in their service. We ourselves purchased a boy whom we afterwards brought to Europe, and who gave proofs of the happiest natural disposition. This child, who learned several languages in a short time, told us in the sequel in what manner he had been carried off with several of his brothers and sisters, while they were all at play in a garden.

Harvest, January 1874
Marianne North

About Silsilis they were harvesting their dourra (millet), rather a dwarf variety, but the heads well filled. They generally cut the ears off first, and then the straw, but some people cut down the whole plant at once, and in all cases they thresh it out on the spot. Camels and donkeys were eating their fill of it, and there seemed to be much shedding and waste of the grain, though the straw did not look ripe.

The threshing process was very picturesque; two buffaloes and three cows we saw in one place driven in a circle over the dourra, while a boy with a rake gathered back the ears which had been pushed out of reach of the animals' feet; the beasts were muzzled—an unnecessary precaution, as there were plenty of small boys with nothing to do but to look after the cattle, all the younger children being unclothed because of the heat.

Lupins, with blue and white flowers, were the common crop of the Nile mud close to the water's edge, and looked very pretty. Wheat was also a good deal dibbled in on such spots, with a kind of broomrape growing amongst it, no doubt a parasite, as all of that family are. The date palms often grew in clusters of seven or more from one root-centre, and their curves and feathery tops were most elegant.

Nubia and Beyond

Taking advantage of the wind from the north, travelers pushed on past Luxor toward Nubia. South of Aswan, before the building of the dam at the turn of the twentieth century, travelers had the alarming experience of being taken through the First Cataract. Then came the much loved island of

Philae, other temples and the villages of Nubia, and the great excitement of reaching the vast temple of Abu Simbel.

Approaching Nubia, 1861
M.L.M. Carey

As we approach the scenery of the cataracts, very fine palm-trees again greet the eye, the hills begin to assume a darker hue, and the sandstone gives place to the granite rock. A few Roman ruins crown the top of the hills on the eastern bank as we proceed. On the western, the sand of the desert lies thickly strewn upon the rocks. Here was the island of Kubanieh, and the home of our Reïs. He landed, and was surrounded by a very respectable body of black relatives, for they are Nubians; and before parting he left a basket full of presents for his mother. Each man of the crew, whose home lay on our way, was allowed to pay it a visit, and to rejoin the dahabëëh at the next village at which we stayed for the night. These people never meet their friends empty-handed, and Mohamed had provided a large box to contain his presents for his friends. They were frequently handsome, such as a fez, some coffee cups, or a silk-handkerchief, and he received many in return, in the form of dates, sugar-canes, and sheep.

At half-past four P.M., *Saturday, Dec*. 15*th* we reached Assouan, the ancient Syene; and here 'Cousin Phil' and the whole party turned out for a walk. I sat on the bank fishing, Mohamed squatted at my side, musing and meditating on the lovely romantic scenery, and on the remains of past glory and grandeur.

But I must not forget the beautiful approach to Assouan. Here begins the actual rocky scenery of the Cataracts, and river appears enclosed as in a basin, or like the opening of a harbour, with lofty hills on either side. The island of Elephantina is in front, and small islands, with the most brilliant patches of vegetation, stud the water. Palm-trees, sont, young barley, and lupines of brilliant emerald green growing on every little scrap of earth (the deposit of the river), between the picturesque masses of granite and porphyry, of which the islets are composed.

In some cases a great number of large, ancient stones are heaped up, as though placed there in preparation for a building; in others they stand erect, singly, and covered with hieroglyphics. Here they assume all kinds of fantastic shapes, human figures, skulls, or old castles; there they are cut into huge plain blocks bearing the marks of the wedges used to detach them from the larger mass, and lying about as though waiting to be laid in the spot for which they were originally designed. Some of these masses are of enormous size, and we noticed one which had every appearance of having been destined for an Obelisk.

The Nubian Women, 1827
Wolfradine Minutoli

We began by visiting the charming Isle of Elephantina, covered with groves of palms, and a luxuriant vegetation. The complexion of the natives, after having passed through gradations of colour, was, at Syene, of a black and chocolate hue. The women of Nubia do not veil themselves with the same strictness as the Egyptians. The young girls wear a small apron, with leather fringes, and adorned with shells. They are very ingenuous and simple in their manners; and any infraction on the established laws is punished by the father of the family with the utmost rigour.

The Nubians grease their hair in a very disagreeable manner; they use for this purpose oil obtained from the plant called Palma Christi, which they cultivate with much care, and which we found growing round all their huts; they then divide their hair in an infinite number of small tresses, so tightly braided that they generally last for their whole life. Hence we may easily judge the neatness of the head-dress. Like the negresses, they have a taste for tinsel and glass beads.

When we landed on the island of Elephantina, the women and children flocked about us with a cordiality which we had not before met with: they eagerly brought us many little antiquities which they had found on the island, in exchange for which we gave them glass beads, knives, and small looking-glasses, for which they expressed their satisfaction by a thousand demonstrations of joy and gratitude.

The most perfect confidence was soon established between us; they chatted and laughed together, showing two rows of teeth as white as ivory. The figure of the young women appeared to me charming; their skin was

as soft as satin, in spite of the burning sun to which they
are constantly exposed. I believe that the oil with which
they anoint their hair and part of their bodies, contrib-
utes to produce this effect. I had occasion to admire their
courage, for I saw several of them cross the Nile sitting
astride upon the stem of a date tree, with an oar in their
hands, without appearing to be afraid of crocodiles; who,
by seizing one of their legs, might easily have dragged
them to the bottom.

Aswan, 1844

Countess Hahn Hahn

Goods sent by water from Wadi Halfa to Cairo must be unloaded in Messid and again shipped in Assuan, after camels have conveyed them from one harbour to another. Gold-dust, elephant's teeth, and ostrich feathers are the principal articles of commerce from the interior of Africa; so we are informed by a French merchant who is established in Assuan, and who has just returned from Dongola with a caravan of six and forty camels (all his own), whither he had carried European wares of every possible kind—stuffs, implements, glass and bronzes. The black slaves are another and important article of merchandise.

Camels in these countries are invaluable beasts; without them merchants and travellers could not stir. I acknowledge their merits, but I am heartily glad that I have no longer occasion to avail myself of them. Here, as in Messid, they lie in large numbers on the banks of the river, with bales of goods about them, close to the tents or huts of palm leaves in which the owners or the drivers live, until arrangements are made for the further journey. What genuine oriental pictures! The merchants sitting with their pipes under palm-trees, the extended camels, the bales of goods with spices and other fine things; down by the shore, the vessels with their long sail-yards; and then the Nile with the black rocky masses of Elephantina, Bab and Philae! Or there advances, perhaps, a caravan of slim, swarthy Nubians, whose deep-red turbans and white shawls, thrown round the head and shoulders, very well become them. . . .

Philae, with its double pair of entrances, with the long columnar porticoes, with the various temple-halls, which at first are free and open, but the nearer you approach the interior, the holy of holies, become darker and more secret—Philae could witness even now, if the rubbish were removed, some portions completed, and the magnificent ascent from the Nile by the obelisk restored, the celebration of the mysteries of the great goddess to whom the temple was dedicated. It is still, in the midst of its devastation, distinguished by such solemn and sublime a character, that its figures of gods, with sparrow-hark heads and horns of cows, appeared to me, in connexion with them, like the feverish and sickly dreams of a great and mighty spirit.

Face to Face with Africa, 1907
Norma Lorimer

Moslem Assouan is delightful, as all unspoilt Moslem things are. It has an Arab cemetery, which lies in exquisite solitude alone in the desert. It was this Arab cemetery, which did not come into Cooks' tourists' programme of the day ashore, which told me that there were sweeter and better things in Assouan than all the Greco-Roman remains of dynastic rock-hewn tombs in Nubia. I saw this cemetery only for a few minutes, but it took me into the heart of the Moslem world. For a brief moment only I was alone with the sky, death, and the desert—a stolen moment in which I travelled far beyond the margin of the world, deep into the kingdom where thought loses itself in infinity. This little cemetery told me that Assouan is not composed of one huge hotel and a street full of ostrich-feather shops. It showed me

that if you turned your back on the Nile and that most
entrancing view, which in spite of its golden shores and
waving palms does not speak to you of Egypt but of
some dream-place which has no sacred link with the
past, you will find yourself face to face with Africa, with
unclaimed Africa and "golden-treasured Nubia."

Stretched out before you lie the white-domed tombs
of sheikhs, as graceful in the new brilliancy of the tropics
as the fairy kiosks of Aladdin's palace, yet sad with that
tender sadness which hovers round lonely desert tombs;
and beyond them, in the valley, the great caravan route
of the desert, which is no less than the ancient bed of the
Nile. Along this road, if you wait but one half-hour, you
will see a strange procession of travellers—a procession
which will show you that you are very deep in Africa,
that the Nubia which you hoped to see is here!

The Adventure of the Cataract, 1882
Sophia de Franqueville

Today we ought to have finished the first cataract, but
after two hours' work our eighty men decamped with

their Sheik as they were tired! Rather provoking when another hour would have finished their business; but they kindly promised to return with two hundred tomorrow and do *all* the rest of it! The *all* is a quarter of an hour's walking distance.

Yesterday at cock crow all our possessions on deck were cleared, the doors locked etc. . . . Then our own crew retired to the stern, and the pilot of the Cataract took possession of the rudder; the captain of the Cataract was in command; and the bows swarmed with

Cataract sailors, and a very obstinate old Sheik super-
vised the whole. Soon blacks were swimming round the
dahabeeyah for 'baksheesh' on queer rafts: their performance over, business began.

Our feluccas went to fetch men from the shore, and
they were divided into companies on different rocks.
Where they came from, I can't imagine, as they all suddenly hopped up and the banks were like a rabbit warren,
swarming with men, old, middle-aged, young and boys.
They shout, scream, talk, row, but that is almost all.

Ibrahim says, in tones of disgust: "I don't like these
Cataract people at all! All noise—not do any work."

The sand on our right and left is in quite bright
golden heaps banked up. The rocks are, I think, basaltic, bare of any vegetation, only in the shallower pools
there are large tufts of rushes. The chief cause of excitement consists in the tracking rope getting entangled or
the end of the mast being struck against a rock. Oh! the
shoutings, shriekings, howlings, and gesticulations! the
boundings and leapings and flyings! It is simply kill-
ing, and such a farce. . . . The pace at which the river

goes is tremendous, not rushing down but rushing in eddies, whirling one another in the fastest of valses, and in and out the river the folk go; one couple rushing past another and as smoothly as possible. It is an enchanting scene and very fascinating to watch.

The Temple of Isis, 1855
Lady Tobin

We re-entered the boat, and after passing through what is called the *third gate* of the Cataract, landed on the sacred isle of Philae. A short but steep ascent up a wooded bank led us to the great temple of Isis. This superb relic of an era when Philae was held in peculiar sanctity as one of the reputed burial places of Osiris, is considered by the learned as an elegant specimen of the lighter Ptolemaic architecture. It is in truth a noble ruin! The paintings upon the walls of the inner chambers—the sculpture and the painting of the columns and outer walls—still remain as perfect as they were thousands of years ago, and seem destined to be the admiration of ages and ages to come! Here we behold, portrayed to the life—human figures—animals—and the customs and ceremonies of bygone days; with their undeciphered tales in clearly traced hieroglyphs! A staircase leads to small chambers in the wall of the eastern adytum; but a hurried glance was all we had to spare for what—even according to *tourists' rules*—ought to occupy four days. Some of the ceilings are painted dark blue, with white stars, to represent the heavens. We walked along the gallery extending from the propylon to the water's edge, and which *rests* upon a wall that formerly surrounded the island as a protection from the current. The view from hence, as indeed from every part of Philae, is very fine. The temple of Esculapius, with its columns and doorways yet perfect, stands at the end of the eastern corridor in front of the great temple. The whole island is covered with mounds and ruins of ancient edifices, whose fragments appear amongst the mud hovels and scanty vegetation of the present day. Little more than an hour's pleasant row before sunset, by the Western Channel as it is called, to Assouan, brought us back in safety to our river *home.*

The Tropic of Cancer, 1873
Amelia Edwards

About half way between Kalabsheh and Dendur, we enter the Tropic of Cancer. From this day till the day we repass that invisible boundary, there is a marked change in the atmospheric conditions under which we live. The days get gradually hotter, especially at noon, when the sun is almost vertical; but the freshness of the night and the chill of early morning are no more. Unless when a strong wind blows from the north, we no longer know what it is to need a shawl on the deck in the evening, or an extra covering on our beds towards dawn. We sleep with our cabin-windows open, and enjoy a delicious quality of temperature from sundown to sunrise. The days and nights, too, are of equal length.

Now, also, the Southern Cross and a second group of stars, which we conclude must form part of the Centaur, are visible between two and four every morning. They have been creeping up, a star at a time, for the last fortnight; but are still so low upon the eastern horizon that we can only see them when there comes a break in the mountain-chain on that side of the river. At the same time, our old familiar friends of the northern hemisphere, looking strangely distorted and out of their proper place, are fast disappearing on the opposite side of the heavens. Orion seems to be lying on his back, and the Great Bear to be standing on his tail; while Cassiopeia and a number of others have deserted *en masse*. The zenith, meanwhile, is but thinly furnished; so that we seem to have travelled away from one hemisphere, and not yet to have reached the other. As for the Southern Cross, we reserve our opinion until we get farther south. It would be treason to hint that we are disappointed in so famous a constellation.

The Temples of Nubia, 1851
Emily Hornby

Went up to the temple [of Dakkeh] about eight; others were there already.

An inner chamber with two lions, very like those at Mycenae, near the ground, another lion and baboon higher up. This temple is sacred to Thoth, who is represented as a baboon. More baboons in the main hall. Went with Ibrahim to the top of the Pylon, sixty-nine steps. A most exquisite view, river winding a good deal in both directions. Some very curious hills on the Arabian side, might be pyramids, look quite volcanic. Bought some beads here.

On pretty briskly to Maharaka seven miles further. A most lovely row of columns, and a ruinous Pylon, with a relief of Isis sitting under a fig-tree. . . .

The next day we made very good progress and Abou Simbel began to appear about two o'clock. The others could see the colossal figures long before I did. They are most wonderful. The smaller temple of Nefertari comes first; we anchored just below the large one which has four colossal figures of Rameses II in front, two on each side of the doorway, all the temple itself excavated out of the solid rock. One of them has lost its head which is lying at its feet, the others are most perfect, beautiful calm features and lovely ears which are really three feet long. The doorway is approached by a corridor balustrade on each side covered with chains of captives,

Syrians on the right, Ethiopians on the left; and next to the doorway on the sides of the thrones of the nearest Colossus, beautiful figures of Nile deities twining wreaths of lotus. Inside eight Osiride pillars, very superior to those at Gerf Hassan, pedestals much lower, faces almost perfect. . . . A smaller hall beyond and an inner sanctuary with four colossal seated figures, but too dark to see them.

Then went round . . . trying to see the wonderful things on the wall with candles. I could hardly make out anything. Then Ibrahim and I went to the other temple which has six huge figures, standing, four of Ramses II, and two of his Queen Nefertari in whose honour he built this temple. Here I could also see nothing of the interior decorations. Returned to the large temple and was delighted to see preparations for tea, which we all enjoyed thoroughly, on a table from the *Helene* just in front of the temple.

Then M. and I started up the huge mound of golden sand between the two temples. It was very soft and one had to drive one's feet deep in not to slip back. Ibrahim and one of the men followed us and helped us towards the end. There were a few easy rocks, and we were upon the level of the desert, quite dark stones. M. saw a cairn and said she should go to it, I thought I would not at first, but she seemed to get there so quickly I followed her, and it was delightful walking, quite level and over flat fragments of dark red stone. Most splendid view, the windings of the Nile for miles, it disappeared and then appeared again, and boundless desert on each side; the air too delicious. Coming down was an affair of a very few minutes, and we stopped for a good look at the Colossi, when on a level with their calm unmoved faces. It was nearly dark when we got down. . . .

M. had seen in the guide books that about sunrise was the best time for seeing the temples, so I made an effort, though without much hope, and was actually off before the others, and in the temple soon after six, not waiting for any breakfast. Most thankful I am I did, I could not believe it, the effect was magical. The sun poured right into the inner sanctuary, there were four Deities sitting in silent majesty, their faces rather defaced. All different crowns, one especially a very tall one, the crown of Upper Egypt.

A Mighty Abode, 1907
Norma Lorimer

It is a mighty and awesome sanctuary—a mighty abode of an almighty god.

At the beginning of each new day the sun penetrates the darkness of the temple and illuminates it right up to the very sanctuary. It is at sunrise only that the darkness of the four great halls is broken; it is at sunrise only that the whole building is suddenly lit up as though with a thousand lamps. The light is the light of the sun-god who carries in his advent the promise of Horus.

If you sit in the temple of Abou Simbel in the stillness of the dawn, with the might and majesty of the building enfolding you like the waters of a silent sea, and there await the coming of the sun, you will see the hawk-headed Harmachis step forward from his niche above the door to greet the god as he mounts the bank of golden sand.

Slowly he will pass under the great porch, which is guarded by four kingly figures, and enter the pillared hall, deep-bellied in the rock. There he will walk between the sixteen giant statues of Osiris, which are lined up like a royal bodyguard along his route to the shrine. At the holy of holies Ptah, the ancient god of Memphis, and Amon and Rameses and Harmachis are all seated in expectant attitudes awaiting his coming. In the great stillness you can feel his presence like the presence of a king in whose being there is all majesty, power and dominion.

The beauty of Abou Simbel is its simplicity—its simplicity and strength. Its simplicity humbles and exalts you, its strength overwhelms you. It is its simple majesty that places it as high above other temples made by man's hands as the heavens are high above you.

The Furthest Point, 1847
Harriet Martineau

The next morning was almost as cold as the night; but we preferred this to heat, as our business today was to ride through the desert to the rock of Abooseer—the furthest point of our African travel. Before breakfast, the gentlemen took a short walk on shore, being carried over the intervening mud.

They saw a small village and a school of six scholars . . . The lesson was from the Koran; and the master delivered it in a chanting voice.

Two extremely small asses were brought down, to cross with us to the western bank. We crossed in a ferry boat, whose sail did not correspond very well with the climate. It was like a lace veil mended with ticking. Our first visit was to the scanty remains of an interesting old temple near the landing-place.

We rode to the foot of the rock of Abooseer, and then ascended it—in rather heavy spirits, knowing that this was to be our last look southwards. The summit was breezy and charming. I looked down the precipice on which I stood, and saw a sheer descent to the Nile of two hundred feet. The waters were gushing past the foot of this almost perpendicular crag; and from holes of its strata flew out flocks of pigeons, blue in the sunshine. . . . The whole scene was composed of desert, river and black basaltic rocks. . . . To the north-east, the river winds away, blue and full, between sands. Two white sails were on it at the moment. From the river, a level sand extended to the soft-tinted Arabian hills, whose varied forms and broken lights and shadows were on the horizon nearly from the north round to the southeast. These level sands then give place to a black rugged surface, which extends to where two summits, today of a bright amethyst hue, close the circuit of vision. These summits are at a considerable distance on the way to Dongola. . . .

There is a host of names carved on the accessible side of Abooseer. We looked with interest at Belzoni's and some few others. We cut ours with a nail and a hammer. Here, and here only, I left my name. On this wild rock, and at the limit of our range of travel, it seemed not only natural, but right to some who may come after us. Our names will not be found in any temple or tomb. If we ever do such a thing, may our names be publicly held up to shame, as I am disposed to publish those of the carvers and scribblers who have forfeited their right to privacy by inscribing their names where they can never be effaced.

The time arrived when we must go. It was with a heavy heart that I quitted the rock, turned my back on the south, and rode away.

Crocodiles!, 1873
Amelia Edwards

Our pilot leaned forward on the tiller, put his finger to his lip, and whispered—"Crocodilo!" The Painter, the Idle Man, the Writer, were all on deck, and not one believed him. They had seen too many of these snags already, and were not going to let themselves again be excited about nothing.

The pilot pointed to the cabin where L. and the Little Lady were indulging in that minor vice called afternoon tea.

"Sittèh!" said he, "Call Sittèh! Crocodilo!"

We examined the object through our glasses. We laughed the pilot to scorn. It was the worst imitation of a crocodile that we had yet seen.

All at once the palm-trunk lifted up its head, cocked its tail, found its legs, set off running, wriggling, undulating down the slope with incredible rapidity, and was gone before we could utter an exclamation.

We three had a bad time when the other two came up and found that we had seen our first crocodile without them.

A sandbank which we passed next morning was scored all over with fresh trails, and looked as if it had been the scene of a crocodile-parliament. There must have been at least twenty or thirty members present at the sitting; and the freshness of the marks showed that they had only just dispersed.

Down the Cataract, 1874
Marianne Brocklehurst

Up at six, on deck, boarded by the Reis and his men, the *shellaleen*. As our old Reis remarked, "Twenty to row, thirty to scream and ten to direct."

They row us gently down to the head of the cataract, which is no sham this time, and a different passage to the one we came up. We saw before us a narrow passage between high granite rocks where the water is regularly roaring for about three hundred yards and with a sudden rush and a bound we are in for it.

The great boat gathers fresh impetus every moment, the very Arabs forget to scream for some moments, and just at the last, when we seem to be tearing straight down upon the wall of rocks before us, the steersmen (four of them) give us a good twist and we turn sharp to the left and escape with our lives. The Arabs then gave themselves up to extravagant demonstrations of joy, seized the turbans of some of our men, and salaamed and shook hands with us. They began these manifestations rather too soon and by getting in front of the pilots, who could not see, we narrowly escaped a great rock in the middle of the rapid towards the end, which as it was we bumped and scraped against considerably and might have got a very similar hole in our side to that the poor crocodile had. After this grand go, we sailed in smooth water for some minutes and then had another rush down another rapid, not so long nor so sheer as the first but sufficiently dangerous, as was proved by the dahabeeyah *Dongola* which followed us and got a great hole through her on the rocks of this second rapid, causing a stoppage of two days for repairs before she could be brought to Assouan. We, more fortunate, were now well over our troubles and we glided pleasantly down to Assouan in an hour and a half. The scenery is of course very striking and grand and the morning sunlight made it beautiful.

Northward down the Nile

In the days of sail the travelers' boats had been driven south by the wind from the north. When the time came to return, their boats were carried northward by the flow of the river. On the journey north, more time was allowed for stopping, and they

moored at the towns and the great sites on the banks that they
had passed wistfully as they sailed south to Nubia.

North from Aswan, 1855
Lady Tobin

We were under weigh during the night, and soon after
breakfast reached Komombo—where we remained twenty-
four hours, to give the Reis an opportunity of seeing his
wife and children, who resided there. We walked to the
famous Temple over a strip of parched ground, between
the cracks of which lupins were sprung up—and along the
edge of a field which some Arabs were preparing for cultivation. Near this field was a fine cotton plantation, where
several Nubian slaves—the happiest of Egypt's population,
for they are generally well treated and have nothing to
lose—were busily employed.

The Temple of Komombo is still for the most part
embedded in the sand. It was founded in the reign of
Ptolemy Philometer, and is singular among the exist-
ing temples of Egypt in having a double entrance and
two parallel sanctuaries. Among admirably preserved

sculpture and painting on the walls, friezes, and columns of this majestic ruin, one ceiling attracted our notice from its extremely distinct and fresh appearance—the colours retaining all their pristine brilliancy. Close by, towering above the river, is an edifice erected upon an artificial platform. It is now in so a ruinous state that very little can be traced of its original plan.

On the evening of Friday, November 11th, we anchored at Edfou. We saw during the day three crocodiles and some storks.

A few minutes' walk early the next morning—through fields of millet, beans, lupins, and *bamiahs*—brought us to a wide canal, across which we were safely carried by three of our sailors, who contrived to make a capital *arm-chair* with their hands and arms. We had to pass a manufactory of earthen jars, and along a street of the miserable town of Edfou, before we found ourselves in front of the Temple so worthy of its fame.

From the summit of the massive gateway we looked down upon the noble court (now used as a granary) with its yet perfect rows of columns—and the rich fertile valley of the Nile. The river here makes a very considerable bend.

Kom Ombo, 1844
Countess Hahn Hahn

We visited [the temple of Kom Ombo] towards sunset, and the purple rays majestically illuminated it, as candelabra light up a catafalk. Later rose the moon, causing the lovely forms even more distinctly to step forth, the ruins to sink back in deeper gloom, and giving the broad desert the aspect of a winding-sheet; add to this, the solid silence all around, and the tranquil Nile softly flowing at our feet, and you have one of the finest pictures which this journey has yielded me.

You would like to hear something of the temple itself. Only conceive! The ante-hall alone stands upright, and in such a way that pillars are buried in the sand to the half of their height. The four rooms which follow it are lost up to the frieze, and the cross-beam stone blocks, twenty to twenty-two feet in length, have sunk down. In order to look closely at the hieroglyphics, the designs, and the well-preserved colours, I knelt upon the sand which reaches above the door-cornice, and found upon the frieze remarkably well-wrought escutcheons of the time of Ptolemy.

The Almé Dancers, 1861
M.L.M. Carey

[At Esna] the streets of the present town are almost on a level with the roof of the portico [of the temple], and the wretched hovels of the natives are built so close upon the beautiful ruins that they hide them completely. . . . In the evening we went with Mohammed to what he called 'a private house' that we might see the 'almé' dance. The 'private house' was little more than a mud hovel. The space in which the girls danced could hardly have been five foot square; the spectators, mounted on the raised seat against the wall, were seated on their own chairs, which had been brought with them from the boat. A bed with mosquito curtains was at one extremity of the apartment; a divan at the other. The instrumental and vocal performers crowded at the little open door-way; and a

small oil lamp, hanging from the ceiling, was the only light provided, to illuminate the darkness. Had we not brought our own lantern with us, little indeed should we have seen of the performance. The 'almé' dance with their bodies rather than their feet, making a series of contortions, shakings and joltings, which suggest the idea that the figures of these girls consist of two distinct parts, which have very little to do with one another.

They shuffle their naked feet along the ground in a most inelegant manner, keeping time to the music which is being played for them. One of the girls played with small brass cymbals, a pair of which she held in each hand; her companion raised one hand to her head, at times as though in grief, at others spying through her fingers with most impudent looks, while the other arm was fixed akimbo on her side. There were regular figures to the dance; the performers seemed to follow the music according to their own inclination, and at the conclusion of the exercise they looked as hot and tired as might be expected after such unnatural exertions. . . .

The dress of the 'almé' is always gay and handsome. They wore on this occasion striped India silk, and necklaces of gold coins, crocodiles, and other forms, all in gold. Their fez caps were sewn all over with small money; a handsome crown piece of solid gold fastened the rich black silk tassel; and a number of long braids of silk, equally covered with coins, forty of them at least, dangled behind the tiny plaits of their black hair, which between the silk braids and the tassel of the fez, were very little seen.

We were sufficiently pleased with these curiosities to be enabled to express truthful admiration and satisfaction, notwithstanding the sensations of disgust and pity which the dancing itself could not fail to raise in a European lady's mind. We were glad to have seen it, but were equally sure that we should never wish to witness it again; though the fiddler and his fiddle we would most gladly have captured and taken away with us.

Honest Sarah's sense of propriety received even a greater shock than ours, and her looks of undisguised horror were an amusing part of the play: indeed I am not sure that they had not their effect in increasing the impudent looks of the 'almé,' which were towards the conclusion mostly aimed at her. But Sarah could not get over a great number of the daily sights she saw in this strange land, as her averted eyes and frequent sudden disappearances into the depths of the cabin abundantly testified. But we will not quarrel with her for this; it is a fault on the right side. And we like her all the better for her true English modesty.

Delays and an Accident, 1858
Emily Hornby

Got up early for El Kab, and then heard there was not time for us to stop there, as the tug was bound to be at Luxor this evening, which we had never understood. However, there was no help for it, and personally, I was not sorry, as I had rather a cough, and was glad of a quiet day. Passed Esneh. Quite an important town, with some good houses, evidently belonging to Europeans, and a railway station. Temple rather hard to distinguish, there is so little of it above ground. A great many palm-trees about. Several dahabiehs anchored, and a good deal of shipping. On the opposite side, the Arabian side, a range of pale pink hills. Expected to be at Luxor about four. Meant to dine at hotel and have quite a festive evening, but twice got upon sand-banks, and were a long time getting off, so soon that was hopeless.

Finally, about seven, just before dinner, heard loud yells on deck, and then a tremendous crash. Quite thought the crew had mutinied, and that we were going to be murdered; but Ibrahim rushed into the saloon, saying,

"Ladies, do not be frightened!" It appeared the tug had insisted on going on after dark, against advice, got upon another sand-bank, and pulled us after her right upon another boat already stranded there, with a large anchor hanging outside. The anchor had gone right through the side of the saloon, and across the corner into M.'s cabin. She was lying on the bed, and it must have gone within an inch of her head. We cannot be too thankful for such a providential escape. We now anchored for the night; the broken glass was cleared away, and we were left with half one side of the saloon open.

Such Great Heat, 1862
M.L.M. Carey

We emerged from the sepulchres into the open air under the broiling sun, and finding just sufficient shade to accommodate us beneath the wall of the rocky entrance, we spread our shawls on the sand, and sat down to luncheon. The Arabs would taste nothing, because it was Ramadán: even a little boy to whom an orange was offered put it away until the evening feast.

The degree of heat which we experienced here would in an English climate have induced extreme languor and loss of spirits; but the bracing air of Egypt produced a totally different effect. Although the exposure to it was at times painful, or even dangerous, inducing headaches and burning feverishness in those with whom it did not quite agree, yet we never felt languid during any part of our journey, and we noticed an unusually even flow of spirits in all the travellers on the Nile, not excepting the invalids.

Back in Cairo, 1854
Lady Tobin

We bade adieu to our dahabieh on Thursday, December 8th, and drove in an open carriage to Shepheard's Hotel. It was market day at Boulak. An immense number of loaded camels were standing or lying in an open space to our left, and we passed many more on the road. The hotel is the largest I ever saw; with its handsome stone staircases, wide corridors, and lofty apartments. There are good baths too, and a well supplied *table d'hote*. On the other hand, the beds are by no means so free from *creeping things* as they might be with proper care, and the attendance is woefully deficient. Certainly what *we* call good servants must be extremely scarce in Egypt.

The constant arrival of passengers to and from India keeps up an unceasing bustle and excitement. Young and old, married and single, black *ayahs* and English nursery-maids, sickly squalling children, yellow faces and dowdy dresses, disappointed hopes and ardent expectations— all assemble here! Of mere *tourists,* the Americans are at present the most numerous. They leave their own country with a fixed resolve to *see* so much and *spend* so much within a specified time, and almost invariably perform to a hair's breadth what they have undertaken.

Returning North to Alexandria, 1850
Florence Nightingale

We did not get to Atfih till ten o'clock, too late to bid adieu to our solemn old Nile; who, indeed, had been all that day as ugly and as contrary as it was possible to be. It was pitch dark. We had heaps of luggage. Nobody helpful but S. There was the wretched sick woman to be carried. Mrs —'s spoilt child would not part from its wax doll. What was to be done? A good-natured man took charge of the doll and the child, and I took charge of his baggage, as being the least helpless thing of the two, and of Mrs —.

At last we arrived at the Mahmoudieh Canal—you have to walk across to the boat as they do not open the locks at night. If anybody could have drawn that scene, how good it would have been. The imperious old Smyrniot, with her blue cockade in the foreground, the miserable Benczik, with the Zizinia dog in his arms, which it became a *tour de force* to be able to hold, behind—helpless females not daring to step across the plank. At last Mrs — and I were left alone on the shore. Paolo came. "Take Mrs —," I heroically cried; "I will not stir from the hatbox of the man who has taken charge of the doll." Oh! If you could have seen the whole scene!

Adieu to Cairo 1874
Marianne Brocklehurst

Adieu to Cairo. After all our wanderings we look back upon it as the most enchanting city in the world, with its narrow streets, its party coloured mosques and minarets far sweeter than those of Constantinople or Damascus, its shady, gleamy bazaars and motley coloured crowds. We shall never see the like again! Oh Cairo!

We journey together by train to Alexandria, are very sleepy and very cross with an ugly-looking fat Egyptian who gets in unexpectedly. We try to turn him out with the help of Abas [their dragoman] and don't succeed. He turns out indeed to be Governor of Alexandria and talks English as well as we do. He brought the first hippopotamus to England, he says, and we become very friendly in the long run, and very well we do perhaps!!

Luxor and Ancient Thebes

As today, after Alexandria and Cairo, most travelers' main experience of Egypt is in Luxor—on both the east and the west banks. However, many travelers in the days of sail stopped only briefly at Luxor when going south, spending a much longer time there and on the west bank while sailing

north—carried along by the flow of the river toward the end of their time in Egypt.

Arrival at Thebes, 1817
Sarah Belzoni

We at last reached Luxor. Still there was no rest for the soles of our feet. There was no boat to take the great colossal head on board; and, notwithstanding this poor accommodation, we were obliged to set off for Gheneh. We had no sooner arrived there than we were obliged to return, as there was a large boat pressed for the use of the Bashaw, wherein some Franks had taken their passage as far as Aswan, which boat was promised for Mr B. for the head. We tied our little boat to the large one. We had come down well enough with the stream in our miserable bark; but on going against it we had not set off twenty minutes when the Arabs began to cry out most dreadfully: in a moment we found the boat was half full of water. Fortunately the large boat, perceiving our danger, ran to land immediately, and we went on board of it.

The next morning we arrived at the wished for haven. Mr B. had but just time to put me in a house, where he was informed that there would be a room on the top for me; he was then obliged to sail for Esneh to secure the boat.

This was the first time I had ever been left alone with the Arabs without an interpreter or a European, with about twenty Arab words in my mouth. What they denominated a room, consisted of four walls open to the sky, full of dates put to dry in the sun, an oven in one corner, a water jar, and a fireplace of three bricks for a pot to stand on, without a chimney; and this place not to myself, as it was an apartment for the women. I never in my life felt so isolated and miserable, in a violent fever, exposed to the burning sun; beside the torment to have all the women of the village coming out of curiosity to see me.

At last I began seriously to think of enclosing one corner of this place for myself: fortunately it happened to be market day; I sent to buy some mats, and with the help of the women (I was going to say), who did more harm than good, I made me a comfortable little room, inclosed and covered over; I had all my things taken in. Beside the pleasure to be by myself, I had the additional luxury of two ounces of tea, which I had received from Cairo on the return of a courier. I felt more content at that moment than I now should in the finest palace of Europe.

I had just begun to enjoy a little repose, when I had an attack of opthalmia. During the first ten days a virulent humour discharged from my eyes; I had not any thing to apply to them: I could not bear the light. I used to filter the water to wash them. Whenever the women saw me washing them with water they would all set up a cry telling me it was very bad, and that it was my washing them every morning that had made them so. In Nubia they had the same idea.

My eyes were determined not to be cured so easily: blest with the comforts of Job, the women told me in twenty days perhaps I might get better; but if not in that time, it would go on for forty days—and finished by crying *Malash* (no matter). Instead of being better at the end of twenty days, I became totally blind. I cannot describe the agony I felt on the occasion; I thought I had lost my sight for ever. My situation was not an enviable one, the women still crying *Malash*. The last stage of the disorder was truly dreadful; the eyelids lost their power, I could not lift them up; this was another blow. The women boiled garlic in water to steam my eyes over: it is possible it might have done some good, though I did not feel the effect immediately. I found their experience in this matter perfectly correct; the eyelids began to gain strength, and by degrees, at the end of forty days I could see a little. After getting well of this attack, I made it a rule to wash my eyes daily with water mixed with aqua vitae, which strengthened them much: if ever I found them inclined to a relapse, I made the wash stronger, and kept washing them several times a day: it never failed to cure them; though I never had my eyes as strong as they had been before.

Luxor Temple, 1843
Countess Hahn Hahn

We had seen the temple of Luxor in the morning, and we had it besides always before our eyes, since it lies close upon the Nile, consisting of three halls of columns—a

colossal one, and two smaller—which produces a grand
effect at a distance, as well as when you are near to them.
Viewed at a distance, particularly from the other bank,
and by the light of evening, with the Arabian mountains as background, and the broad and silent Nile as
foreground, these pillared halls have the mythologi-
cal character of a picture by Claude Lorraine. You do
not know to what point of earth it actually belongs, so
dreamy is the vapour, so ideal the colouring, with which

it is enveloped—and yet one is firmly persuaded that upon the earth it may be found.

Standing close to Luxor you are doomed to behold its charms disappearing before the most loathsome of loathsome realities. By the side of this obelisk, which is and will remain the admiration of all times, which is wrought in granite with the delicacy and sharpness of a cameo— by its side, and amongst the four granite colossi and pylons—that royal entry to palaces and temples, as far as the end of the pillared halls, the village has nestled, crept and built itself up; it is an abomination to wind one's way through such filth. What a desecration of pillars, temples and sacred things! Under such circumstances, to be buried more than half in rubbish is an advantage. The obelisk is free. It was probably dug out when its companion was taken to Paris. I have driven perhaps twenty times along the Place de la Concorde, and that obelisk has always appeared to me to overload the spot rather than ornament it. Now I know why. Egyptian architecture is from one casting. If its columns and pylons, and the whole arrangement of the building, are rendered palpable to the senses, energy, endurance and strength, so do the obelisks, elevating their slim forms as monoliths, sixty, seventy, eighty feet high, elegantly and distinctly, by the side of those mighty and dark forms, show that strength may have also grace. . . .

I rejoice that I had the good taste not to fall into ecstasies at the obelisk in Paris because it drew its origin from Thebes. There it is utterly unfitting, as it is here in harmony with all that surrounds it. Two colossi are buried up to the breast, two even to the covering of the head. The pylons looked as if decaying; a mosque, and a children's school—in which boys were very assiduously reading, with a measured rocking movement of the upper part of the body—are leaning against them.

Trade in Antiquities, 1874
Amelia Edwards

Forgers, diggers, and dealers play, meanwhile into one another's hands, and drive a roaring trade. Your dahabeeyah, as I have just shown, is beset from the moment you moor till the moment you pole off again from the shore. The boy who drives your donkey, the guide who pilots you among the tombs, the half-naked Fellah who flings down his hoe as you pass, and runs beside you for a mile across the plain, have one and all an 'anteekah' to dispose of. The turbaned official who comes, attended by his secretary and pipe-bearer, to pay you a visit of ceremony, warns you against imposition, and hints at genuine treasures to which he alone possesses the key. The gentlemanly native who sits next to you at dinner has a wonderful scarab in his pocket. In short, every man, woman and child about the place is bent on selling a bargain; and the bargain, in ninety-nine cases out of a hundred, is valuable in so far as it represents the industry of Luxor—but no farther. A good thing, of course, is to be had occasionally; but the good thing never comes to the surface as long as a market can be found for the bad one. It is only when the dealer finds he has to do with an experienced customer, that he produces the best he has.

Flourishing as it is, the trade of Luxor labours, however, under some uncomfortable restrictions. Private excavation being prohibited, the digger lives in dread of being found out by the Governor. The forger, who has nothing to fear from the Governor, lives in dread of being found out by the tourist. As for the dealer, whether he sells an antique or an imitation, he is equally liable to punishment. In one case he commits an offence against the state; and in the other, he obtains money under false pretences. Meanwhile the Governor deals out such even-handed justice as he can, and does his best to enforce the law on both sides of the river.

The Unrivaled Ruins of Karnak, 1859
Emily Anne Beaufort

The more fortunate chance would be to have a fine moonlight view after becoming well-acquainted with the plan of the ruins; but even under the disadvantage of seeing what we did not properly understand, it was a scene that impressed itself upon the mind for ever; the deep black shadows concealing much of the brokenness and decay, and the splendid light illuminating, with a sort of tender glory, the massive columns, immense pylons, and slender obelisks. By this light it was only and altogether

beautiful and lovely; but one needs the sunshine and blue sky to bring out the stupendous proportions of these unrivalled ruins.

Perhaps few spots on earth could be more solemnly beautiful than the centre aisle in the Great Hall, with the six gigantic columns between the sixty-one attendant columns on either side, the moonlight piercing through the open clerestory of delicate tracery against the dark sky, turning the obelisk, ninety-two feet high, at one end of the aisle, into a silver needle, rising with a stern grace against the ruined temple behind it; and at the other end

illuminating a single column, standing alone in the centre of a vast square, between giant pylons and huge walls,
with its capital complete, its shaft uninjured, seeming
almost livingly sorrowful in its loneliness.

Last Scenes at Luxor, 1847
Harriet Martineau

The finest impression, or the most memorable, which we
obtained at El-Karnak was derived from our moonlight
visit, that last evening. There is no questioning of any
style of art, if only massive, when its results are seen by
moonlight. Then, spaces and distances become what the
mind desiderates; and drawbacks are lost in shade. Here,
the mournful piles of fragments were turned into masses
of shade; and the barbaric colouring disappeared. Some
capricious, but exquisite lights were let in through crev-
ices in the roof and walls of the side chambers. Then,
there were the falling columns and their shadows in the
great hall, and the long vistas ending in ruins; and the
profound silence in this shadowy place, striking upon the
heart. In the depth of this stillness, when no one moved

or spoke, the shadow of an eagle on the wing above fell upon the moonlit aisle, and skimmed its whole length.

It was with heavy hearts and little inclination to speak that we turned, on our way home, to take a last view of the pylons of Karnak. The moonlit plain lay, with the river in its midst, within the girdles of the mountains. Here was enthroned the human intellect when humanity was elsewhere scarcely emerging from chaos.

"Belzoni's Tomb," 1824
Anne Katherine Elwood

I thought of Aladdin and his cave, as from a painted corridor we passed into a room filled with spirited sketches, and then by another staircase we found ourselves in a large subterranean hall, and a handsome arched room, where stood the alabaster sarcophagus. One of the lateral apartments has a projection all round, and was termed from thence by Belzoni 'the side-board room:' it was, when first discovered, full of small figures of perfumed wood, from six to ten inches long, covered with hieroglyphics, many of which are still remaining. The walls of all are covered with the most spirited paintings, the colours as fresh and as vivid as if finished yesterday, and it was with difficulty that we could believe they were some thousand years old.

One room is in an unfinished state, and, from this circumstance, is, perhaps, more startling and affecting than those which are completed, for it has the appearance of having been just left by the workmen, who were intending shortly to return to complete their performances. There was something wonderfully striking, and even awful, in thus traversing these majestic suites of subterranean apartments, excavated in the bowels of the earth; and I really could have fancied myself visiting some of the palaces of the Arabian Nights, constructed by magicians or genii.

Our Arab attendants were highly delighted with all they saw, and one of them, who had particularly devoted himself to me, and insisted on being my squire wherever I went, amused us considerably by his way of doing the honours. He was particularly pleased with a huge ox in a procession, to which he turned my attention, making a chucking noise, as if to bid it to go on; as Michael Angelo

exclaimed 'cammina' to the equestrian statue of Marcus
Antoninus; and when, after examining the figures with
mature deliberation, he and his companions had discovered their eyes, noses, mouth, &c. with the greatest joy
and glee they pointed them out to us, expressively touch-
ing their own features at the same time, as if doubting
our capacity to comprehend them; and upon some of the
party writing their names upon the wall, they immediately fell to imitating them, by scribbling something also,
as if they thought it was some magical ceremony.

Praise for the Paintings, 1828
Sarah Lushington

The paintings, with colours as vivid as those of any modern artists, and the engravings, in alto and basso-relievo, in perfect preservation did not delight me so much as an unfinished chamber, the walls of which were covered with drawings previously to their being cut in the stone. These were mere outlines in black or red, but sketched with such boldness and lightness, that the more I looked the more I admired. Scarcely can I yet believe the hand that traced them to have been dead so many centuries. Many of the figures are as large as life, and though mere outlines, wrought with as much expression as a finished painting.

No book could better have portrayed the usages of the Egyptians than these tombs. Everything is described: in one chamber, preparing and dressing the meat, boiling the cauldron, making the bread, lighting the fire, fetching water. Another chamber presents scenes in a garden, a boy being beaten for stealing fruit, a canal, pleasure-boats, fruit, flowers, the process of various arts, such as sculpturing, painting, mixing colours, etc.

After seeing two more tombs I was compelled to return home from fatigue.

Mummies, 1828
Sarah Lushington

In the evening, I accepted the invitation of Signor Piccinini, a Lucchese, in the service of the Swedish Consul at Alexandria, who had resided about nine years at Thebes, to see the opening of a mummy, that I might myself take out the scarabaeus, or any such sacred ornament as might be found in the coffin. The Signor's dwelling was nothing more than a mud hut in the hills of Gournoo. I ascended to the only apartment by a few steps; this room contained his couch, his arms, his wine, his few drawings, and all his worldly goods. The window shutters, steps, and floor, were composed of mummy coffins, painted with hieroglyphical figures, perhaps four thousand years old; and it was curious to observe the profuse expenditure of materials to which I had been accustomed to attach ideas of value, from seeing them only in museums and collections of antiquities.

I had accompanied Signor Piccinini with great glee, thinking what a fine thing it would be to tell my friends in England. What my notions of opening a mummy were I cannot define—something, however, very classical and antique—certainly anything but what it proved in reality.

Half a dozen Arabs were standing around, panting under heat, dust, and fatigue. They had only just brought in their burthen, and were watching with eager look the examination of its contents, (their profits depending upon the value of the prize), while the candles which they held to assist the search lighted up their anxious countenances.

The outside case of the mummy was covered with hieroglyphics, and the inner one consisted of a figure as large as life, with the face and eyes painted like a mask. On lifting up this cover, nothing was seen but a mass of dark yellow cloth, which, though it must have consisted of at least fifty folds, yielded like sand to the merciless hand of the operator, and the skeleton appeared to view. It was some time before I could recover from the horror with which the scene impressed me; I saw no more, but this lit-tle was sufficient to make me consider the employment as disgusting as that of a resurrection man, and the manner of performing it not less unfeeling. It may be called the pursuit of science, but to me it appeared nothing more than rifling the dead for the sake of the trifling ornaments with which the corpse is generally buried.

This, indeed, was the fact; for the moment it was ascertained that the mummy contained no ornament, the skeleton, together with the papyrus, on which were inscribed numerous distinct hieroglyphics, and the other materials, was cast forth as worthless rubbish. Sufficient papyrus and relics have been procured for the interests of science; and I think it would redound to the Pasha's credit if he were to issue an edict, to clear his country from these mummy scavengers. He had, indeed, ordered all the corpses to be re-interred; but, according to evident demonstration, this order was habitually disregarded.

Scarabaei are scarce; a few were brought us by the Fellahs, while wandering about the ruins, though none of value. Ancient coins are procurable in abundance, but they are too numerous to prove curious, and they had certainly no beauty to attract us to be purchasers.

Egypt beyond the Nile

The desert stretching on either side of the river and into the Sinai Peninsula makes up a greater part of Egypt than does the fertile land beside the Nile. Not all travelers ventured into the desert—nor do they today—but for those who travel in these dry lands there is a different—and often exciting—experience.

The First Day Out, 1899
Emily Hornby

The Arabs and camels were all crouched round a little Arab village quite near behind a fence of brush wood; some children were about. I had some hot milk and toast for breakfast—it answers better than anything. It was most interesting to see them load the camels. The bedding etc. was all rolled up and put into square sacks closed by a flap. I could fancy Joseph's brothers had that kind. A network of strong rope is laid across the camel, which is kneeling down and grunting very much, a package slung on each side, the ends brought across the camel's back and laced up.

I was perfectly comfortable on my camel. . . . We were each led by a very nice Arab. I have tried in vain to learn their names, I must write them down tomorrow. The whole procession was led by a baby camel which seemed to be quite following its own devices.

We followed the line of the Red Sea, glittering to our right, a line of mauve hills beyond; the desert was exactly like the sea shore, sometimes stones about, sometimes not. To our amazement we saw posts, and heard they were the telegraph line to Sinai. . . . We plodded steadily on for four hours—it was not at all hot—and then pulled up for a halt, on what seemed a peculiarly flat and shelterless piece of sand, but there were some tufts of coarse herbage, not grass, but a sort of little shrub, on which they said the camels could graze. They also handed to me this morning two sorts of yellow flowers, growing close to the ground, which the said camels like very much. The little boys kept gathering bundles and handing them to them.

Our luncheon tent was put up in a second, our saddles arranged as armchairs, and we were thoroughly comfortable. Luncheon followed: sardines, hard-boiled eggs, cold chicken, cheese and pickled onions—which they think a great delicacy, and I am very fond of myself. Onion is bussal in Arabic. Wine and coffee afterwards, oranges and raisins. We rested nearly all the hottest part of the day, but it was still very hot when we started.

No Water in the Desert, 1876
Isabella Bird

The water had been hardly drinkable at noon, and at night, when I asked for rice, Hassan's gloomy countenance grew yet more gloomy, and he said there was not water enough: the Bedaween had stolen it. Being unable to have either rice or chocolate, what I had in the morning having been made of *saltish* water, possibly from Marah, I supped on raisins and chocolate paste only.

Of course there was not any water for washing either that night or the next morning—a discomfort under any circumstances, and an actual hardship in these. When I lay down I asked Hassan to bring me all the water that there was, and he presently reappeared with a most glum and clouded face, bringing a teacup nearly full of a thick, dark-coloured fluid like the refuse stream of a dye-work, and, putting it down by me, said, "You get all; you very ill." Then, smelling it, he said, with a look of infinite disgust, *"Stinks."* I felt as if I could drink up the Nile, and as I raised myself on my elbow frequently during the night and sipped this foetid decoction of goat's hide in teaspoonfuls, the suffering hourly increased. I was really ill and I wondered if I could remain sane until the afternoon of the next day, twenty hours later, when we would reach the wells of the Wady Feiran.

All the watery texts of the Bible came to my memory, and those beautiful words—"A pure river of water of life, clear as crystal" absolutely tortured me.

The Khamsin, 1848
Harriet Martineau

Today we had experience of the Khamsin. When the heat had become so intolerable that all moved forward silently in dull patience, some with a secret wonder whether they should ever breathe easily, or feel any muscular strength again, a strong wind sprang up suddenly from the south. Though it was as hot as a blast from an oven, and carried clouds of sand with it, I must say I felt a great relief. I was aware that the sensation of relief could not last; for the drying quality of this wind was extraordinary, and I immediately felt this upon the skin. Still, the sensations under the evaporation were those of relief for the moment; and before they were over, we stopped, and could get under the shelter of our tents. The thirst which this wind caused was of course great; but we had plenty of water and oranges. I was surprised, after all I had read, to see how like thick fog an atmosphere full of sand can be. The sand was not course enough to be felt pattering upon the face, though it accumulated in the fold of one's dress; but it filled the air so completely as to veil the sunshine, and to hide altogether the western boundary of the wadee, and all before us. The eastern mountains, near whose base we were travelling, rose dim and ghostly through this dry hot haze. We were to have proceeded to the Wadee Gharendel, where there is a small spring and a palm or two; but this wind caused us to halt sooner, for the advantage of a sheltering sandhill.

An Afreet, 1911
Lady Evelyn Cobbold

We make our way through the desert till an opening in the hills shows us the Pyramid of Medum, first seen glowing like a pink pearl against the faint blue sky of evening.

We are once more in sight of the Nile. Beyond the Pyramid, on the other side of the river, stretches the Arabian Desert, and the Mokattam Hills rise like a great amphitheatre, showing ridge upon ridge of deep mauve, yellow, and rose, changing from moment to moment so completely that new mountains and colours seem to replace those just vanished. We camp within a few miles of this relic of a long-past age, older than the Pyramids at Ghiseh, built by King Snefru about four thousand years BC.

Slowly we journey through this mysterious land, whose every grain of golden sand is steeped in history.

Towards nightfall we pass near a large cemetery on the edge of the desert. Our watchman, Reched, being weary and wishing to make a short cut, carelessly walks through it, thereby tempting the powers of evil, with the unfortunate result that in the distance he sees a woman in white. He then knows that an afreet has entered into him. His "blood changes," and from having been a happy, sunny youth, he became dejected, haggard, nervous.

The Arabs realise that he is possessed, but hope, as the afreet has only just entered him, that a holy man will be found with a charm potent enough to exorcise the evil spirit.

All Arabs firmly believe in the existence of these genii or afreets who, as taught by the Koran, are an intermediate order of creatures who eat and drink, live and die, and in many ways resemble mankind. There are good and evil genii, and they can make themselves visible under the guise of animals, and more especially snakes. When passing through dark alleys, graveyards or likely haunts of the evil ones, an Arab will recite a verse of the Koran to protect himself. At the great Day of Resurrection, the genii and animals will appear, as well as men.

The Travelers

136   **ISABELLA BIRD** (1831–1904) was the greatest of Victorian travel writers. From England, she went to America and Canada as a young woman, and later traveled to Australia, Hawaii, and again to America. She went to China and Malaya, and returning from that journey she visited Egypt and went on pilgrimage to Sinai.

96   **MARIANNE BROCKLEHURST** (1832–98) visited Egypt four times between 1873 and 1896 and made a considerable collection of antiquities, now in Macclesfield Museum.

43   **E.L. BUTCHER** (fl. 1914) lived in Egypt as the wife of a churchman. Her insights into the country are added to by photographs at a time when the inundation still flowed through the buildings at Philae, the temple at Abu Simbel was close to the river, and there were many working boats on the Nile.

6, 14, 72, 103, 108   **M.L.M. CAREY** (fl. 1860), writer and artist, traveled cheerfully on the Nile in 1863–64 with her elderly cousin, his

invalid daughter and two English servants. She published
her account illustrated with her lively pictures.

LADY EVELYN COBBOLD (1867–1963) spent much of her   *138*
childhood in Morocco, where she became attracted to
Islam. She spent periods in Egypt, particularly the Fay-
oum, and went officially on pilgrimage to Mecca as a
Muslim.

LUCIE DUFF GORDON (1821–69), owing to ill health,   *35*
lived for a time in South Africa and then in Egypt, where
she died and was buried in Cairo. She lived in Luxor and
became very much a member of Egyptian society there.
She wrote regularly to her family, and these letters were
published both in her life and after her death.

AMELIA EDWARDS (1831–92) was a writer who first visited   *85, 94,*
Egypt in 1873–74, publishing a good account of her jour-   *120*
ney. Fascinated, but disturbed, by the casual exploitation
of Egypt's past, she became deeply involved in Egyptol-
ogy, working for the creation of the Egypt Exploration

Society to carry out disciplined research in exploring and recording the standing monuments.

15, 57, 125

ANNE KATHERINE ELWOOD (fl. 1840) accompanied her East India Company employed husband to India, traveling through Egypt in 1825–26. When they returned to England she wrote about her journey and her life in India, as well as an important book about women authors.

8

ELIZA FAY (1756–1816) was a very adventurous woman. She accompanied her husband to India in 1799 through Egypt and the Red Sea. They separated, but she worked on in India on various business ventures.

80

SOPHIA DE FRANQUEVILLE (1852–1915) was the daughter of the Lord Chancellor of Great Britain. She traveled through Egypt and on through Sinai to Petra and Syria.

24, 77, 102, 117

COUNTESS IDA HAHN HAHN (1805–80) was a divorced German aristocrat and novelist who traveled in the Near East with a male companion in the mid-1840s. She converted to Catholicism, established a convent in Germany, and lived there for the rest of her life.

EMILY HORNBY (d. 1906) traveled to Sinai and Petra in 1899 and 1901, and sailed the Nile with her sisters in 1906. Her journal of this Nile journey was published by her sisters as a memorial to her.

NORMA LORIMER (1864–1948) traveled on her own through North Africa and Egypt in 1907. Her account of that journey is described in her diary.

SARAH LUSHINGTON (d. 1839) was the wife of an Indian army officer with whom she traveled through Egypt on their return to England, giving guidance for ladies intending to brave the 'Overland Route.'

HARRIET MARTINEAU (1802–76) suffered from ill health and deafness but this did not stop her becoming an important economist and traveling widely in America in

1834–36 and the Near East in 1848—often showing her interest in the economy of the country.

26 **E.M. MERRICK** (fl. 1900) was a portrait painter who, in Egypt, painted the American journalist–explorer H.M. Stanley. She went to India and became a successful artist there.

67, 74 **WOLFRADINE MINUTOLI** (1794–1868), as a young bride, accompanied her Prussian husband on a scientific mission to Egypt, and published her account of the journey in English in 1827.

16, 110 **FLORENCE NIGHTINGALE** (1820–1910) visited Egypt with friends and possibly there took the momentous decision to train as a nurse—a profession thought unsuitable by her parents. Put in charge of nursing during the Crimean War, Florence became a great heroine.

69 **MARIANNE NORTH** (1830–90) was a traveler with a good sense of humor and one of the most intrepid of the

'Victorian lady travelers.' She traveled with her widowed father until he died in 1869, then she set off around the world to paint as many of the plants of the tropics as she could find. Her work is on display in a special gallery in London's Kew Gardens.

IDA PFEIFFER (1797–1858) was born in Vienna. After *30* an unhappy marriage and motherhood, she set out to travel in 1842, first to the Holy Land and Egypt, then to Norway, Brazil, Chile, China, India, Baghdad, Constantinople, Cape Town, Borneo, New Orleans, and London.

SOPHIA POOLE (1804–91) was the sister of the Arabist *36, 39,* Edward Lane. She lived with him and her two sons in *45, 61* Egypt for many years and published *The Englishwoman in Egypt* when she returned to England.

ISABEL ROMER (c. 1805–52) separated from her husband *60, 66* and traveled in the East, and published an account of her travels in two volumes in 1846.

1, 21, 53, **LADY TOBIN** (fl. 1840–60) visited the Middle East twice
83, 100, with her husband. She wrote and illustrated an account
109 of their first journey.

33, 63 **MARY WHATELY** (1824–89) was the daughter of the Arch-
bishop of Dublin, where she worked among the poor,
particularly in schools. In the early 1870s she went to
Egypt and set up schools for poor Egyptian girls, traveled
as a missionary on the Nile with her Syrian colleagues,
and wrote several books about her experiences.

Bibliography

Beaufort, Emily Anne. *Egyptian Sepulchres and Syrian Tombs*.
   London: Longman, Green and Roberts, 1861.
Belzoni, Sarah. "Mrs Belzoni's Trifling Account," in Giovanni
   Belzoni, *Narrative of Operations and Recent Discoveries*. London:
   John Murray, 1828.
Bird, Isabella. "A Pilgrimage to Sinai," in *The Leisure Hour*. London,
   February–April, 1886.
Brocklehurst, Marianne. *Miss Brocklehurst on the Nile: Diary of a
   Victorian Traveller on the Nile*; repr. Disley, Cheshire: Millrace,
   2004.
Butcher, E.L. *Things Seen in Egypt*. London: Seeley Service, 1914.
Carey, M.L.M. *Four Months in a Dahabeeh or a Narrative of a Winter
   on the Nile*. London: Booth, 1863.
Cobbold, Lady Evelyn. *Wayfarers in the Libyan Desert*. London:
   Arthur L. Humphreys, 1912.
Duff Gordon, Lucie. *Letters from Egypt*. London: Macmillan, 1875.
Edwards, Amelia. *A Thousand Miles up the Nile*. London: Longmans
   Green, 1877.
Elwood, Anne Katherine. *Narrative of a Journey Overland to India, and
   a Voyage Home 1825-8*. London: Colbourne and Bentley, 1830.

Fay, Eliza. *Original Letters from India.* Calcutta: Thacker, Spink and Co., 1908.

de Franqueville, Sophia. *On the Nile.* London, 1889.

Hahn Hahn, Countess. *Letters from the Orient or Travels in Turkey, Egypt and the Holy Land.* London: J.C. Moore, 1845.

Hornby, Emily. *A Nile Journal.* Liverpool: J.A. Thompson and Co., 1908.

———. *Sinai and Petra: The Journals of Emily Hornby in 1899 and 1901.* London: James Nisbet and Co. Ltd, 1902.

Lorimer, Norma. *By the Waters of Egypt.* London: Methuen and Co., 1909.

Lushington, Sarah. *Narrative of a Journey from Calcutta to Europe.* London: John Murray, 1829.

Martineau, Harriet. *Eastern Life, Present and Past.* Philadelphia: Lea and Blanchard, 1848.

Merrick, E.M. *With a Palette in Eastern Palaces.* London: Sampson Low, 1899.

Minutoli, Wolfradine. *Recollections of Egypt.* London, 1827.

Nightingale, Florence. *Letters from Egypt 1849–1850.* Edited by Anthony Sattin. London: Barrie and Jenkins, 1987.

North, Marianne. *Reminiscences of a Happy Life.* London: Macmillan, 1898.

Pfeiffer, Ida. *Voyage to the Holy Land, Egypt and Italy.* London: Ingram, Cooke and Co., 1853.

Poole, Sophia. *Letters from an Englishwoman in Egypt.* Edited by Azza Kararah. Cairo: The American University in Cairo Press, 2016.

Romer, Isabel. *A Pilgrimage to the Temples and Tombs of Egypt, Nubia and Palestine.* London: Richard Bentley, 1846.

Tobin, Lady Catherine. *Shadow of the East.* London, 1855.

Whately, Mary. *Letters from Egypt to Plain Folks at Home.* London, 1879.

———. *Among the Huts in Egypt: Scenes from Real Life.* London: Seeley, Jackson, and Halliday, 1871.